OCD WORKBOOK FOR ADULTS; WORKBOOK FOR MANAGING OCD USING COGNITIVE BEHAVIORAL THERAPY, EXPOSURE THERAPY, MINDFULNESS AND ACT

Mike Abraham

© Copyright 2021 by Shark publication. All right reserved.

The work contained herein has been produced with the intent to provide relevant knowledge and information on the topic described in the title.

This statement is legally binding as deemed by the Committee of Publishers Association and the American Bar Association for the territory of the United States. Other jurisdictions may apply their own legal statutes. Any reproduction, transmission, or copying of this material contained in this work without the express written consent of the copyright holder shall be deemed as a copyright violation as per the current legislation in force on the date of publishing and the subsequent time thereafter. All additional works derived from this material may be claimed by the holder of this copyright.

The data, depictions, events, descriptions, and all other information forthwith are considered to be true, fair, and accurate unless the work is expressly described as a work of fiction. Regardless of the nature of this work, the Publisher is exempt from any responsibility for actions taken by the reader in conjunction with this work. The Publisher acknowledges that the reader acts of their own accord and releases the author and Publisher of any responsibility for the observance of tips, advice, counsel, strategies, and techniques that may be offered in this volume.

Table of Contents

Introduction   **9**

Chapter 1: Definition and Symptoms of OCD 12

What Is OCD?
Symptoms of OCD
Obsessions
Symptoms that You Have Obsessive Thoughts
Symptoms that You Have Compulsive Behaviors
Symptoms of OCD in Children

Chapter 2: Causes of OCD   **20**

What Causes Obsessive-Compulsive Disorder?
Personality
Personal Experiences
Biological Factors
Unstoppable Impulses
Serotonin System
Genetics
Cognitive-Behavioral Theories

Chapter 3: Why Has Nothing Worked?   **30**

Why Is Your Medication Not Working?
How to Cope With It?

Why Is Psychotherapy Not Working for You?
How to Cope With It?
Strategies to Fight With Treatment-Resistant OCD
Combination Therapy and Pharmacological Treatment
CBT
Further Options

Chapter 4: Types of OCD   37

Scary Obsessions
Compulsions OCD
Contamination OCD
Responsibility OCD
Perfectionism OCD
Harm OCD
Sexual Orientation OCD
Pedophilia OCD
Relationship Themed OCD
Scrupulosity OCD
Hyperawareness OCD
Emotional/Mental OCD
Action OCD
Fear OCD
*Heal*th OCD

Chapter 5: Treatment Options   56

Psychological Therapy
Cognitive-Behavioral Therapy (CBT)
Imaginal Exposure
Habit Reversal Training
ACT (Acceptance and Commitment Therapy)
Other Treatments
Augmentation Therapy
Repetitive Transcranial Magnetic Stimulation
Deep Brain Stimulation
Electroconvulsive Therapy
Brain Surgery

Chapter 6: Self-Assessment   68

Chapter 7: Cognitive Behavioral Therapy or CBT for OCD   74

What Is CBT?
Cognitive Behavioral Therapy Types
Impact of Cognitive Behavioral Therapy
Benefits of Cognitive Behavioral Therapy
CBT Techniques Used for Treating OCD
ERP (Exposure and Response Prevention)
How Is ERP Different From Traditional Psychotherapy (or Talk Therapy)?
Exposure Ritual Prevention and Awareness Exercises
Cognitive Therapy
Metacognitive Therapy

Strategies of Cognitive Behavioural Therapy for Treating OCD

Chapter 8: Imaginal Exposure Therapy 110

What Is Imaginal Exposure Therapy?

Facts About Writing Stories of Imaginal Exposure

Chapter 9: ACT and Mindfulness 126

Mindfulness

Deep Breathing

ACT – Acceptance and Commitment Therapy

Why Choose Acceptance and Commitment Therapy for the Treatment of OCD?

WORKBOOK EXERCISE

Accepting Emotions

Chapter 10: Other Methods of Treatment 144

Chapter 11: How to Sustain It for the Long-Term and Not Fall Back? 146

Eat Good Food

Don't Avoid Your Fears

Don't Be a Black-and-White Thinker

Follow Your Prescriptions

Be Patience With Your Progress

Maintain a Journal
Avoid Chasing Perfectionism
Conclusion

Introduction

Obsessive-compulsive disorder, or more commonly OCD, is a type of mental illness that is known to cause unreasonable, excessive, or unwanted sensations or thoughts over and over again. The urge to do some activity repeatedly is one of the most common characteristics of this mental illness. Many-a-times, individuals suffering from OCD may possess both compulsions and obsessions. Now, you may have a bad habit of biting nails or rethinking negative thoughts. So, you might have thought that you are suffering from obsessive-compulsive disorder. But, you are wrong in this case, as such habits are not the symptoms of OCD. Have you observed any of your close ones possessing the fear of getting affected by germs, as well as the requirement or urgency of arranging scattered objects in a particular manner, etc.? If yes, then that person is having some symptoms of this mental illness. But, you need not worry at all. With the help of proper medical diagnosis and necessary treatment, OCD can be controlled.

Unpleasant thoughts are something that we all experience at some point of time or the other. But how will you understand that the root cause of these thoughts is OCD and not something else? We are going to discuss the symptoms of OCD in detail in this book but here, I am going to give you a brief intro.

What do you understand by intrusive thoughts? Something that is unwanted and comes into your head all of a sudden and can also lead to distressing feelings, right? These thoughts are not based on any particular topic. They can be about anything and everything. Another characteristic feature of these intrusive thoughts is that they leave your mind very quickly. They don't linger. And these thoughts do not characterize a person to be bad or evil.

But when these intrusive thoughts are because of OCD, they are usually more serious and come more frequently. They tend to make the person worried to greater degrees. Moreover, they don't leave quickly. They will stay latched onto your mind until you figure out how to calm yourself down. A very significant property of such thoughts is that they tend to revolve around things that can bring devastating and great consequences to the person's life, which naturally makes them panic even more. But for this person, it might seem an impossible task to deal with such intrusive thoughts.

In this book, we will learn more about OCD, how you can identify it, what are the treatment options you have, and also how you can sustain your recovery. Keep on reading if you want to know more!

There are plenty of books on this subject on the market, thanks again for choosing this one! Every effort was made to ensure it is full of as much useful information as possible.

Part I

Chapter 1: Definition and Symptoms of OCD

Are you constantly thinking about something you don't even want to think about? Are you doing things repeatedly and feeling powerless to just stop? Chances are you must be suffering from OCD. In this chapter, I am going to talk about what OCD is and what its symptoms are.

What Is OCD?

OCD or Obsessive-Compulsive Disorder is a type of mental illness responsible for causing unwanted sensations and thoughts (obsessions) repeatedly. You may also get an urge to do something repeatedly (compulsions), even if you don't want to do it. Some OCD patients have compulsions, some have obsessions, and some have both compulsions and obsessions.

Habits like negative thinking or nail-biting have got nothing to do with OCD if done willingly. Considering some colors or numbers to be "good" or "bad" might be an example of obsessive thinking. An example of compulsion is washing your hands eight times after you touch something that you consider dirty. Even if you want to stop, you feel powerless and keep repeating until your brain believes that you have done it a "good" number of times.

Even people suffering from OCD are aware of the fact that their sensations and thoughts make no sense. It's not that they enjoy them or something. It's just that they have no power over it. Quitting seems impossible, and they keep repeating the same things unwillingly. When they finally stop, they don't feel good and start doing it again.

Repetitive thoughts or habits are a common thing for everyone. But it is OCD if your actions and thoughts:

- Interfere with your social life, work, or any other aspect of your life.

- Are not something you enjoy.

- Are something you can't control even if you want to.

- Consume a lot of your time.

Symptoms of OCD

OCD symptoms rarely happen all at once. Its symptoms start so small that you may think of them as normal behaviors. But when something negative happens to you, like a loved one's death, abuse, or any personal crisis, these symptoms might get triggered. OCD symptoms include compulsions, obsessions, or both.

Obsessions

An uncontrollable fear or thought that induces stress is known as an obsession. Some examples of obsessive thoughts are:

- You are constantly suspicious that your partner is cheating on you, even when there is no proof to justify that.

- You are constantly aware of breathing, blinking, and other bodily sensations.

- You constantly worry about other people or yourself getting hurt.

- You fear using public toilets, touch doorknobs, or even shake hands with other people.

Symptoms that You Have Obsessive Thoughts

- You are afraid of germs and dirt. You are so afraid of getting yourself dirty that you don't want to touch objects like doorknobs or even people who have touched these objects that you consider to be "dirty." You don't even want to shake hands with other people, or hug them, or come to any sort of physical contact with them.

- You feel the extreme necessity for maintaining order. You are so obsessed with having everything in order that you exhaust yourself, making sure that everything is in place and according to your plan. When objects are a little out of order, you feel so stressed that you can't even concentrate on any other work until you make sure that everything is back to order again.

- You constantly have a fear of hurting others or yourself. Even if the thing you are thinking about is totally different, you suddenly start getting thoughts of hurting others or yourself. For example, you imagine yourself walking on a bright and fun day, and then suddenly you have thought of getting involved in an accident or falling somewhere in the road, etc. No matter how hard you try not to think about that part, it still comes to your mind.

- You have an excessive amount of fear or doubt about committing a mistake. You constantly need some sort of reassurance or encouragement from other people, who would tell you that whatever you are doing is okay or right. If someone constantly tells you that yes, you will be able to do it, you feel a little better. But if other people don't reassure you, you get scared of making mistakes, and you start panicking so much that you actually end up making mistakes.

- You fear embarrassment. You are scared that you might not be able to socialize or gel in perfectly with the crowd. You are scared to speak because you fear saying something vague and stupid. You distant yourself from serious or heated conversations because you fear that you might say something stupid or bad. You get so conscious to prevent yourself from all the embarrassment that you actually end up embarrassing yourself.

- You fear hostile or evil thoughts. This includes warped ideas about religion or sex. You constantly imagine troubling scenarios. It may be some disrespectful situation or maybe some troubling sexual scenario. Whatever it is, it's extremely unbearable, but you can't help it from invading your mind.

Compulsions

If you repeat an action or a ritual a lot, then that is termed as a compulsion. Some examples of compulsive behaviors are:

- You always get the urge of counting things like bottles or steps

- You do a task repetitively until you feel you did it a "good" number of times

Symptoms that You Have Compulsive Behaviors

- You can't stop yourself from cleaning or washing. You keep washing your hands again and again; you keep taking a bath or a shower again and again, or you keep cleaning objects repeatedly. You keep rinsing your hand to the extent that your skin gets all raw and chapped.

- You can't stop checking. You repeatedly keep checking everything you just did. For example, you just locked your doors and are going out. You are not able to leave until you check your lock 6-7 times, even when you know that you just locked it and checked it. Another example is, suppose you just finished cooking and you are wrapping up. You are not being able to leave your kitchen because you are just going on checking whether you turned off all the kitchen appliances, whether you closed the fridge door, whether you turned off the chimney light. You are going to sleep, and you check whether you turned your washroom lights repetitively.

- You can't stop counting. You keep saying numbers to yourself out loud in a certain pattern.

- You want everything to be in order. You feel the necessity to eat a particular food in a particular order. You want to arrange the items in your kitchen pantry or your clothes in a particular order. If a single thing is out of order, you start getting anxious. Your top priority becomes bringing that thing into order again. No matter how urgent your other works are, you will keep everything on standby just to have everything in "proper" order.

- You stress a lot about routines. You keep doing or saying things in a particular way until you feel you have done it a set number of times. Only after doing that are you able to leave the house.

- You keep hoarding or collecting. You have a lot of unnecessary things in your home which you don't even ever use, but you still find it impossible to stop yourself from collecting or buying more of them. For example, suppose you have a lot of clothes and shoes, but you still can't stop shopping even if your wardrobe has no more space!

Symptoms of OCD in Children

The initial signs of OCD can start appearing in adolescence. Sometimes, they can even start appearing in childhood. Some symptoms of OCD among children are:

- The child faces trouble in maintaining or forming relationships and friendships

- The child developed some sort of physical illness that developed from stress

- It is difficult for the child to complete his or her school work

- The child fails to follow the routines

- The child has low self-esteem issues. He gets nervous while talking to someone, or gets overwhelmed in someone's presence, etc.

OCD in childhood is more common in men than in women. In adulthood, men and women get affected at a similar rate.

It is not a light matter and needs serious treatment. A lot of people experience these symptoms and think there is no need to seek help, but that is totally wrong. It is a serious disease and must be treated carefully.

If not treated, the symptoms may grow severe over time, making your life miserable. You need to get some blood tests done and maybe a physical examination to make sure that these symptoms are not caused by any other factor.

Once the tests are done, the doctors can now clearly diagnose OCD. There is no particular cure for it, but certain therapies and medications can help bring your symptoms under control. Some popular treatment methods include Transcranial Magnetic Stimulation, Neuromodulation, medication, relaxation, etc. Yoga, exercise, and meditation also help to some extent.

Chapter 2: Causes of OCD

OCD or Obsessive-Compulsive disorder is a type of mental illness, as a result of which people experience certain repetitive, unwanted sensations or thoughts (obsessions) or the urge of doing something again and again (compulsions).

Some OCD patients experience only obsessions, some experience only compulsions, and some experience both obsessions and compulsions.

An OCD patient might experience some obsessive thought that leads to compulsion. As a result, that person starts doing something over and over again until he or she feels that it has been done a "good" number of times.

Some people keep checking whether or not they turned off the light switches, whether or not they turned off the appliances, whether or not they touched something dirty, whether or not they locked the doors before leaving their house, etc. It's not that the people suffering from OCD enjoy these things.

They also know that this is stupid and that it doesn't make any sense, but still, they can't help giving in to these compulsive behaviors.

It's like they know what they are doing is not healthy, but still, they feel powerless to quit doing it. In this chapter, I will be talking about the various causes that might induce OCD.

What Causes Obsessive-Compulsive Disorder?

The cause of OCD is often a mystery. This is because patients keep struggling to understand what is actually causing this disorder. OCD patients are already over thinkers, and in addition to that, some patients believe that if they are able to find out the root cause of their disorder, they might be able to fix the disorder.

These patients are often seen to spend hours trying to figure out the cause of their disorder. Some patients claim that their OCD got triggered because of some particular life event. Some of the common triggering events are doubtful interactions, cannabis use, traumatic experiences, etc. Well, it is actually true that some past events can really induce symptoms of OCD in people, and it is even observed in cross-cultural OCD studies.

There are different theories about what actually causes OCD. Although none of them can fully explain the experiences of the person, according to researchers, these are probably involved in inducing OCD. These are:

- Personality
- Personal Experiences
- Biological Factors
- Unstoppable Impulses
- Serotonin System
- Genetics
- Cognitive-Behavioral Theories
- Psychodynamic Theories

Personality

Certain researches indicate the fact that people with certain personality traits are prone to develop OCD. If you are a methodical, meticulous, or neat person with very high standards, you are likely to develop OCD.

Personal Experiences

According to some studies, OCD might be rooted in some personal experiences in your past life. Some examples are:

Some painful childhood experiences, bullying, abuse, or trauma might have caused the onset of OCD in you. You might have learned these compulsions and obsessions as means of some defense mechanism for coping up with all the anxiety caused by that situation.

You might have witnessed your parents do the same things. If your parents also had anxiety issues and you witnessed their compulsive behaviors, it is possible that you learned all those as a coping technique.

There might be some ongoing stress or anxiety in your life. If you are going through some stressful events in your life, like joining a new job or an accident, it can be the triggering event for OCD. It can even worsen the already-existing OCD.

Pregnancy can also induce OCD in some people. Sometimes, when you are about to start a new journey in your life, or when your life is going to witness a huge change, or when you are going to have a lot of responsibilities soon, OCD can get triggered.

Biological Factors

According to some biological theories, when your brain lacks a chemical known as serotonin, it might have an important role in inducing OCD. It still isn't clear whether it is a cause of OCD or is an after-effect of it.

Researches have also been conducted to find out how various parts of the brain might have something to do with causing OCD, but nothing constructive has been found yet.

The biological theories about the onset of OCD are studies about the circuit relay system, which is present between the orbitofrontal cortex and the thalamus.

The orbitofrontal cortex is responsible for all your complex behaviors like reward-based decision making, evaluation, emotion regulation, and goal-directed behaviors.

The orbitofrontal cortex's loop circuits include some other regions like the basal ganglia's caudate nucleus. This is associated with certain functions like voluntary motor movements and cognition.

On activation of these circuits, your attention goes towards these impulses. As a result, you perform a certain behavior, which is directly addressing the impulse.

Let me give an example: Imagine you just used the washroom and you start washing your hands to remove all the harmful germs that you got on your hands. Once you wash (the appropriate behavior for that impulse), your brain circuit diminishes. As a result, you stop washing your hands and carry on with your day.

Unstoppable Impulses

When you have OCD, ignoring or turning off these impulses from your brain circuit becomes impossible. As a result, you have compulsions or repetitive behaviors and obsessions, or uncontrollable thoughts.

For example, your brain fails to turn off the thought of germs on your hands, and you keep washing your hands again and again. Compulsions and obsessions associated with OCD are sometimes related to contamination, aggression, and sexuality.

Your brain circuit is also responsible for controlling these things. Doctors and scientists have observed neuroimaging studies and confirmed the abnormal activities in the brain circuit.

Serotonin System

Some OCD patients respond to certain treatments that include medications like SSRIs (Selective Serotonin Reuptake Inhibitors).

These are responsible for boosting the neurochemical serotonin. This indicates that the dysfunction of the brain circuits might have some relation to the problems associated with the serotonin system.

Genetics

It is believed that OCD might have a genetic component to it. There is a possibility for you to develop OCD if you have a family member who is suffering from OCD. Almost 25% of OCD patients have family members or relatives with OCD.

Some studies have shown that in identical twins, if one of them has OCD, then the other one is also likely to develop the disorder. 45-65% of chances of you developing OCD as a child is based on genetics.

Cognitive-Behavioral Theories

I'm sure every one of you does experience some unexpected or bizarre thoughts throughout the entire day. Cognitive-Behavioral theories of OCD suggest that if you are prone to OCD, then you will not be able to ignore these bizarre thoughts.

Moreover, some OCD patients might even think of these thoughts as dangerous and feel the need to control these.

For example, you might think that you are going crazy because you are having these unexpected and unexplainable thoughts. You might also fear that you would carry out these thoughts that you are having (like hurting your loved ones). Because you label these thoughts as dangerous, you start remaining watchful and vigilant of them. You might constantly look outside your door to check whether or not there is a burglar in your neighborhood.

When you start noticing these thoughts constantly, the danger increases. As a result, a vicious cycle gets created, and you feel trapped inside it while trying to monitor these thoughts. Focusing on something else gets really difficult when you are stuck inside this cycle. It becomes almost impossible to free yourself from these distressing thoughts. This leads to the birth of obsessions.

The hand-washing compulsion might be a learned process. You feel contaminated, you stress about it, you start washing hands, your anxiety reduces, and you feel good. So, this is responsible for reinforcing this behavior of hand-washing. As a result, whenever you experience an obsession, i.e., a fear of contamination, you start acting compulsively, i.e., start washing your hands repetitively in an attempt to reduce your anxiety.

Inclined to Obsess

People who have experienced stressful life events in their past life tend to engage in symmetry and checking compulsions after the onset of OCD.

They may do it as an attempt to impose a certain degree of order in an increasingly unpredictable world.

Although there is a temptation to figure out the actual cause of OCD, it is not always possible to do so. OCD is not something caused by late toilet training, culture, or religion. OCD is caused by a complicated interaction of stressors, personality, environment, and genetics. You can't figure out a particular factor that is causing OCD.

Similarly, it isn't possible to identify a particular gene that is responsible for OCD. Some people take birth with an inclination towards OCD, and then it gets triggered by the combination of their life events.

In some cases, the onset of OCD was bound to happen, irrespective of the circumstances and the life events. Some people remember the onset of some OCD symptoms in their childhood, but in the majority of the cases, the onset takes place in the 20s.

Figuring Out the Cause Isn't Enough to Cure OCD

In some cases, certain traumatic experiences and negative life events may induce the onset of OCD in people. But exploring these events psychologically doesn't ensure anything. You can't cure yourself with these psychological explorations.

These psychological explorations are nothing but treatment approaches, like psychodynamic psychotherapy. It is done for a better understanding of your past life and your subconscious mind, for finding a route to emotional healing. The main goals of these kinds of therapies are to have a better insight and uncover your hidden motivations.

This helps the doctors or the therapists to develop insight-oriented therapies. Having an insight is not enough. OCD patients are likely to be introspective, and they have already spent a lot of time ruminating about the root cause of their disorder. This rumination can also be a type of mental compulsion, thereby worsening the pre-existing symptoms.

Many therapists make this common mistake of leading their patients to ruminate their triggering events, which contributes to worsening their disorder even more. There isn't a single proof that guarantees that if you find out the root of the problem, it is going to give you a solution to fix it. It has been observed over the years that treating OCD patients by psychodynamic approaches are not enough. Some cognitive-behavioral therapists might also get wrapped up in finding the root. The therapist can dig a little to understand the patient better, but it is not the solution to the problem.

The patients must be encouraged to refocus all their energies and efforts on combating OCD through EX/RP (Exposure and Ritual Prevention). EX/RP is a cognitive behavioral therapy that is specifically designed for OCD. Identification of the core fear of the client must not be confused with the search for the root. Identifying the core fear is very important for guiding the appropriate exposure exercises development.

The most important thing that you need to keep in mind is that there isn't any definite cure for OCD. EX/RP is the best possible treatment offered by science, so it is better that OCD patients try this out and try combating their repetitive compulsions and distressing obsessions.

Chapter 3: Why Has Nothing Worked?

OCD is a disorder where people inhibit compulsive behaviors and obsessive thoughts. It can be mild in some people, and in some people, it might be very severe. OCD patients tend to obsess over some thoughts that they don't even want to think.

It is just not in their hands to eliminate those obsessive thoughts.

Some OCD patients inhibit compulsive behaviors such as they keep checking whether everything is in order, counting everything possible, doing something over and over again until your brain thinks that you have done it a "good" number of times.

It's not that people enjoy doing these, but it is just not in their power to control their thoughts, emotions, and actions. OCD, if left untreated, can have a huge negative impact on your life. It must not be taken lightly.

There are different kinds of treatment approaches for OCD (Obsessive-Compulsive Disorder). One-third of the total number of people suffering from OCD develop treatment-resistant OCD.

This means that they don't respond to conventional OCD treatments like psychotherapy and medication. In this chapter, I will be talking about treatment-resistant OCD, why it happens, and how to cope with it.

Why Is Your Medication Not Working?

There are a lot of medications available, approved by the FDA, for treating OCD. For some people (nearly one-third of the total number of OCD patients), those medications don't seem to work.

This can happen for a lot of reasons like taking drugs, consuming alcohol, skipping doses, taking some other medications simultaneously, body chemistry, or genetics. Sometimes, you need quite a lot of time to experiment with various medications and dosages to find out the ideal one for you.

How to Cope With It?

Try considering Augmentation treatment strategies. The treatment of OCD using Augmentation therapy is not just about medication; it is much more than that.

This treatment strategy increases the chances of eliminating OCD symptoms by the use of a combination of drugs and not just one drug.

You can also consider Augmentation antidepressant treatment if you don't see any improvement with a single medication. Antipsychotic drugs can also be added to an antidepressant to check if it works out for you, as it does for some people.

Why Is Psychotherapy Not Working for You?

Psychological treatments are very popular in treating people with OCD. But it doesn't ensure 100% effectiveness. Although most of the patients recover through psychotherapy, some don't. There can be a lot of reasons why psychotherapy isn't working for you like:

- You don't have any family support.

- You don't have any social support.

- The relationship between your therapist and you might be insufficient.

- You are receiving a wrong therapy.

- You are not mentally ready for receiving the therapy.

How to Cope With It?

- Try investigating all those intensive treatment programs. There are a lot of effective psychological and medical treatments available for treating OCD.

- Still, all the treatments are not effective on every patient. There are some patients who don't show any improvement by any of these treatments. As a result, intensive OCD treatment programs evolved.

- You can try clinical trials. Some clinical trials are offered for free. There are some cutting-edge treatments out there that haven't gained much popularity but can be effective for treating patients with treatment-resistant OCD.

- You can go for brain surgery or psychosurgery. There are very few OCD patients who have enough severe symptoms to opt for brain surgery. Surgical procedures related to OCD treatment involve the inactivation of certain regions of the brain that are mainly responsible for causing the symptoms of OCD.

  Almost 50-70% of the people who undergo brain surgery notice significant improvement post the surgical procedure. Deep brain stimulation is an example of neurosurgical procedures that seems to be very effective. It is still in the experiment phase and can be opted as your last resort.

Strategies to Fight With Treatment-Resistant OCD

Here are some important strategies that you should know –

Combination Therapy and Pharmacological Treatment

Augmentation therapies are the first to try after you developed treatment-resistant OCD. Augmentation combined with an antipsychotic proved to be efficient only for a few numbers of people. This was most efficient on people who had a history of maximal SSRI monotherapy for more than 12 weeks.

Recently a meta-analysis was done on second-generation antipsychotic augmentation. It was observed that risperidone was far better than placebo. It was more effective in reducing depression and anxiety. You can continue the ongoing SSRI for three to six months. You can try experimenting with the doses.

Make sure to increase the dose to a level that can be tolerated by your body. You can even switch to some other first-line agent. You can select some other agent from some other drug class and augment the SSRI with it. According to a meta-analysis of OCD SSRIs, the high doses were found to be more effective compared to the low or medium doses. The most significant issue here is your tolerability, which is why this procedure might be a little risky. A high dose of citalopram can increase the risks of arrhythmias, and so a safety warning was raised by the FDA against it.

CBT

Patients generally prefer this. A combination of pharmacotherapy and CBT has shown to be very effective in treating the symptoms of OCD. The interaction between the family members and the patient must be closely observed to find out whether there is covert or overt maintenance of the illness.

Family members should also receive specific instructions about how to behave with the patient, what to say, what not to say, how to act around them, etc. A follow-up should be done too to find out whether they are abiding by all the instructions or not.

Further Options

Among the intravenous administration and the oral administration of drugs, intravenous administration shows much more efficacy in OCD patients.

A study showed that a patient who didn't show any improvement even after receiving many SSRIs showed a 59% response rate after receiving intravenous citalopram.

Intravenous pulse loading seems to be even better at improving OCD symptoms in treatment-resistant OCD patients. We will learn more about treatment options in the second part of this book.

Part II

Chapter 4: Types of OCD

Starting from obsessing over keeping everything clean to checking the lock over and over again before leaving home, there are several types of OCD.

In this chapter, I am going to talk about the different types of OCD, and the different types of behavior people display when they are affected by these types of OCD. OCD is mainly of three types: Obsessive, Compulsive, and Obsessive-Compulsive

Scary Obsessions

Your obsessions can be related to anything. You can obsess over getting some bad thoughts, to the need to keep yourself clean, hurting others, the need for keeping everything in order, etc.

These obsessive thoughts will make you question yourself, but don't get bothered by that. These questions may force you to lose your sanity, calm, and composure. Obsessive thoughts are the thoughts that keep coming to us throughout the entire day. Some obsessions may lead to compulsions as well.

Compulsions OCD

Excessive obsessions may make a person exhibit compulsive behavior as a means of coping mechanism. It just worsens everything.

Compulsive behaviors include excessive praying, avoiding things, washing hands repeatedly, behaving rudely, meaningless aggression, checking things, again and again, to make sure things are right, making sure everything is in order, etc.

Sometimes, people start exhibiting compulsive behavior just to get rid of all the guilt they have been facing because of their obsessive thoughts.

Let me tell you about the sub-types of OCD, often observed in people:

Contamination OCD

If you are suffering from contamination OCD, you tend to obsess over spreading germs or getting infected by an illness. This leads to severe distress and anxiety.

As a result, you become scared of going out to public places. Some patients even hesitate to shake hands with other people.

You will keep washing your hands repeatedly because of the fear of getting contaminated by germs. You may avoid public washrooms, gatherings, etc.

You can become aggressive when someone brings something close to you that you consider to be "dirty." Some patients even fear getting contaminated with other people's bad luck, breath, and negative emotions.

Some common contamination OCD obsessions are:

- You have a fear of developing cancer, contracting STDs, or a fear of getting ill in general.

- You fear that you might spread contaminants and illnesses to others.

- You constantly fear bodily fluids that include semen, saliva, blood, etc.

- You fear dirt, dust, radiation, toxins, germs, etc.

Some common contamination OCD compulsions are:

- You engage in illogical rituals like repeating, knocking, praying, etc.

- You keep researching ailments, illnesses, and germs.

- You tend to scrape off your own skin, fearing that you might be contaminated.

- You start using cleaners containing harsh chemicals for cleaning your skin.

- You change your clothes repeatedly.

- You discard every possible item that you consider "dirty."

- You separate the "dirty" things from the "clean" ones.

- You clean, shower, and wash repetitively.

Responsibility OCD

When you are suffering from responsibility OCD, you are always feeling guilty and anxious about your own actions. You are not at all concerned with your own benefit.

You just keep worrying about the consequences of the things you did and the things you didn't. You will always have a fear of hurting others accidentally.

You may even end up taking all the responsibilities and blames for things that actually have got nothing to do with you. You will constantly blame yourself for everything that is happening around you and may even think that you are a bad person.

There are a few misconceptions about responsibility OCD. People with responsibility OCD often think that the things happening to them are a result of their low self-esteem, or because they care a lot about others, etc.

Some responsibility OCD obsessions are:

- You fear that you won't be able to stop something terrible from happening.

- You fear hurting others.

- You fear putting someone in danger accidentally.

Some responsibility OCD compulsions are:

- You think you are a vicious person.

- You constantly fear harming others by spiritual means, and then you keep praying so that it doesn't happen.

Perfectionism OCD

If you have perfectionism OCD, you will always have a fear of things going wrong. You will always try to make sure that things are perfect.

You want everything to be in order. You are always afraid of what might be the consequences if even a single thing goes wrong.

You always make sure that your or others' performance or behavior is abiding by some particular standard or rule. You will also have a rush and an extreme urge to end something after you have started it, leading to anxiety and hypertension.

If you are suffering from perfectionism OCD, you may find yourself exhibiting the following symptoms:

- You might find yourself repeatedly revising or rewriting personal letters, business letters, project reports, email, classwork, essays, or any work just to make sure they are "perfect."

- You might find yourself redoing all the work and spending too much time on unnecessary details that you fail to meet all your deadlines.

- You might even keep rewriting your sentences just to make them look or sound "perfect."

- You might constantly seek reassurance from others that you did a good job; otherwise, you get anxious.

- You might work for several hours just to finish what you have started, even if it isn't necessary to finish it that time. You just feel unable to leave anything unfinished.

- You keep revising and rethinking your decisions because you simply can't take one.

- You might even avoid completing some assignments just because of the fear of the energy and time needed to make things "perfect."

Harm OCD

Do you often feel like harming or hurting others when you are feeling intense emotions? If yes, then you might be suffering from harm OCD. In harm OCD, patients get aggressive thoughts about hurting or doing something violent to others. If a normal person gets the thought of hurting others while being angry, what would he do? HE would definitely disregard that thought after identifying that it's not right to think like that.

But this is not the case for people with harm OCD. When harm OCD patients get these kinds of thoughts, they start obsessing over the fact that what if they actually do those, what if they lose control, etc.

They start getting engaged in rituals and compulsions to decrease their anxiety. But that is temporary. All the fear and anxiety kicks in again after some time. This is a never-ending cycle.

They need to be constantly reassured that these thoughts are baseless and that they don't mean much.

If you are suffering from harm OCD, these are the symptoms you might have:

- You might get violent images or thoughts in your head and keep worrying that these might come true and thinking that you might do it as well.

- You might worry about hurting others and then not realizing it out of negligence.

- You get terrified thinking that you might intentionally or unintentionally hurt yourself or others impulsively

- You might even think of yourself as a really evil person and that your outer personality is just a cover-up. You keep worrying when your evil side comes out.

Your obsessive thoughts are so frustrating and hard to avoid that you, in order to reduce your anxiety, get involved in rituals and compulsive behaviors like:

- You hide dangerous objects like razor blades, ropes, medicines, poisonous chemicals, kitchen knives so that you can prevent yourself from the temptation of using them against yourself or others.

- You keep reviewing your actions just to make sure they didn't cause any harm to others or to yourself.

- You avoid watching the news and also avoid violent videos, television shows, and movies. This is because you think watching them can trigger your violent side.

- You spend a lot of time researching online about the criminal cases and the offenders to check if they have something in common with you.

- You keep praying and engage in spiritual rituals just to make sure you don't lose control.

- You go on asking people if they think harm OCD patients can hurt others or not.

Sexual Orientation OCD

In this form of OCD, people are afraid of the thoughts of getting attracted to the same sex. They start obsessing over the consequences that they would have to face if they actually develop feelings for the same sex. It is also known as HOCD (Homosexual Obsessive-Compulsive Disorder).

Examples of some symptoms are:

- You keep worrying that your sexual orientation might change.

- You fear people thinking of you as LGBTQ.

- You get scared of your sexual fantasies.

- You keep trying to reassure yourself that you have got nothing to do with LGBTQ.

- You constantly keep checking whether or not you are aroused when you are around other people.

- You keep worrying about what if you don't get aroused when you want to.

- You want to be like everyone else around you.

- You worry about losing control and developing feelings towards a person of the same sex as yours.

Pedophilia OCD

People with pedophilia OCD often get sexual or unwanted thoughts about children. There is a lot of difference between a pedophile and a person suffering from pedophilia OCD.

A pedophile is a person having inappropriate thoughts about children, and they don't even realize that it isn't something good and so they can even engage in inappropriate activities with children, whereas a person with pedophilia OCD is very much aware of the fact that these thoughts are inappropriate and keeps suffering in silence.

Because they know these thoughts are inappropriate, they keep feeling depressed, ashamed, and guilty of their thoughts. These people have no intention of hurting a child, yet they can't help getting those dirty thoughts.

Some common Pedophilia OCD obsessions are:

- You fear that you might have assaulted a young adult or child in the past.

- You fear getting sexually aroused when you are around children.

- You fear getting sexual thoughts about young adults or children.

These obsessive thoughts get so scary for you that you start getting involved in compulsive behaviors to relieve the anxiety. Some common pedophilia OCD compulsive behaviors are:

- You keep researching the legality and morality of getting attracted to someone who is below 18.

- You consider yourself an evil and awful person for having inappropriate thoughts about children.

- You avoid social gatherings where there might be children around you.

Relationship Themed OCD

Having concerns about your relationship or your partner is normal, but if you are obsessing over it the entire day, you might be suffering from relationship OCD.

When you are suffering from relationship OCD, you keep questioning the compatibility between you and your partner, your partner's loyalty, your partner's feelings, and everything else. These doubts are completely unfounded and irrational and can have serious negative impacts on your daily life.

Some common relationship OCD obsessions are:

- You constantly wonder whether or not you are with the right person.

- You are constantly questioning your love for your partner.

- You constantly fear that you are not good enough for being in a relationship with your partner.

Some common relationship OCD compulsions are:

- You set rules for your partner, and if they don't follow those, you think the relationship is not going to work.

- You keep searching for the perfect type of love. Because of this obsession, you can never experience it.

- You get upset during sexual encounters with your partner because you desperately search for passion.

- You keep thinking and questioning your partner's capabilities and qualities.

- You speak to your friends about how their relationships are going to compare theirs with yours.

- You keep researching online what a perfect relationship actually is.

- You notice every small detail within your relationship and keep questioning every small thing in your relationship.

Scrupulosity OCD

People suffering from scrupulosity OCD often get unwanted and intrusive urges, images, or thoughts about violating their ethical, moral, or religious beliefs. As a result, the person starts feeling excessively guilty, anxious, and distressed.

In order to relieve themselves from these feelings, they engage in compulsive behaviors like excessive praying, avoidance, etc. Scrupulosity OCD can be further divided into religious scrupulosity OCD and moral scrupulosity OCD. Let me give you an example of each type.

- **Moral Scrupulosity OCD** – Suppose a person is sitting and conversing with his friends. Suddenly, he makes a joke and nobody laughs! There starts the anxiety. He keeps repeatedly analyzing whether or not he offended someone, or whether his joke was inappropriate, what if people start hating him after this, etc.

- **Religious Scrupulosity OCD (or Religious OCD)** -Suppose a person is attending some sort of a religious service. Some religious dialogues are being read out loud by someone. Suddenly he finds something while hearing it. He starts feeling guilty and ashamed of himself immediately. He starts getting thoughts like what if he ends up in hell, whether or not he is an evil person, whether or not he should confess his fault, etc.

Hyperawareness OCD

People with hyperawareness OCD tend to pay excessive attention to external stimuli. To them, certain things feel to be in greater frequency, persistent, closer, brighter, louder, or more distracting compared to other people.

They don't really want to pay attention to these things, but they feel so distracted by them that they just can't avoid it.

Some common factors that may affect people suffering from hyperawareness OCD are oscillating fans, broken TV pixels, fluorescent light, other people's keyboard typing, screeching brakes, people talking, the noise of others watching TV, highway noise, etc. hyperawareness can be further subdivided, for example, Misophonia (it is a condition where people become excessively aware of external sounds), phonophobia (it is a condition where people fear a particular sound), etc. Some people with hyperawareness often get too obsessive over their own thought processes. They overthink about something, they think about why they are overthinking, and then they feel guilty about thinking what they are thinking.

If you have hyperawareness OCD, your attention goes towards:

- Swallowing in a particular pattern, quality, frequency, and amount.
- The positioning of legs and arms.
- Posture.
- Creaking or popping of joints.
- Feeling of the seams, tags, fit, texture, the weight of the cloth on your skin.
- Sensation, situational context, consistency, and sound of the heartbeat.
- Eye floaters.

- Feeling sound, intensity, and frequency of blinking.

- Fullness, quality, depth, and sensations of breathing.

Some common hyperawareness OCD compulsions include:

- You try not to pay attention to every single detail of everything going around you.

- You try distracting yourself with music.

- You keep yourself occupied all the time and become a workaholic so that you don't pay attention to other unwanted things.

- You try to throw these thoughts out of your mind forcefully.

- You change your whole wardrobe to get rid of certain specific sensations.

- You repeatedly get yourself checked by doctors to see if you have some sort of bodily dysfunction.

Emotional/Mental OCD

People suffering from emotional OCD are always under the impression that nothing is going right. They always feel tense, worried, depressed, etc.

Action OCD

Action OCD is a subtype of OCD, where people think that if they think about something too much, they might end up doing that as well. These people get unwanted thoughts and keep obsessing over the fact that they might come true.

For example, you just got a random thought about a car hitting your partner. If you are suffering from action OCD, you will keep on fearing, obsessing, and questioning whether or not it comes true.

Hoarding OCD

People suffering from hoarding OCD find it very hard to discard possessions, no matter what their actual value is. It has physical, emotional, financial, and social consequences on them and their family members.

They feel that the fact that they have certain things in so much quantity sets them apart from everyone else around them. Some common items to be hoarded are clothing, food, household supplies, photographs, cardboard boxes, plastic bags, paper, magazines, and newspapers.

Fear OCD

Fear OCD involves fearing about getting aggressive thoughts, hurting others, losing control, etc. When people suffer from fear OCD, they feel extremely guilty, conscious, anxious, and responsible for the thoughts they are getting. They often feel they might lose control and do something bad that can have terrible consequences. They often feel that their negligence and carelessness might harm someone severely. If you have a fear OCD, you might have these symptoms:

- You call your partner numerous times a day just to make sure he or she is okay.

- You keep checking all the appliances over and over again just to make sure they are all turned off.

- You keep checking whether or not the door is locked before you leave your house.

- You engage in superstitious behaviors like repeating words, tapping, or counting.

- You wash hands repeatedly and keep cleaning things just to make sure there isn't any kind of contamination.

*Heal*th **OCD**

If you have health OCD, you will have a fear of suffering from some illness, dying, physical or mental suffering, etc. You feel that you can never diagnose what is actually wrong with you and that it is impossible to receive the right treatment. You remain anxious about what will happen if the diagnosis and the treatment go wrong. Some symptoms of fear OCD are:

- Thinking that you are suffering from some illness that is still unknown to mankind.

- Thinking that the doctor might make mistakes while reading your test reports.

- Thinking whether or not your illness is remaining undetected.

- Whenever you feel some sensation, you think of it as a symptom of severe disease.

- Thinking you are at fault for not checking all the symptoms correctly.

- Feeling uncomfortable being around someone who is suffering from some disease.

- Thinking whether or not you missed some crucial symptom that has a direct connection to whatever illness you are suffering from.

In case you have any of these above-mentioned OCD, you should not take it lightly and keep it untreated. OCD can get worse with time, and avoiding it would not do any good. Get yourself treated. There are a lot of treatment approaches available nowadays. Starting from psychotherapy to brain surgery, you can do a lot of things to treat your OCD.

WORKBOOK EXERCISE

What kind of OCD do you have?

_____
_____

Write down the thoughts that you experience when triggered.

_____
_____
_____
_____
_____
_____
_____
_____
_____
_____
_____
_____
_____
_____
_____
_____
_____
_____
_____
_____

Chapter 5: Treatment Options

Among all the patients suffering from OCD, 32 to 70% of patients show remission, thereby proving that recovery is possible. People suffering from OCD can be treated in various ways. In this chapter, I am going to talk about the different treatment options available for curing OCD.

Psychological Therapy

Psychological therapies for OCD effectively reduce the intensity as well as the frequency of the symptoms of OCD. One such example of psychological therapy is CBT or Cognitive-Behavioral Therapy.

Among all the patients undergoing CBT, almost 2/3rd of them notice a significant decrease in the intensity and frequency of OCD. CBT is quite expensive, which is why a lot of people like to receive CBT in healthcare settings or hospitals to cut down the expenses.

So, if you are receiving Cognitive-Behavioral Therapy in such settings, then you have an option of receiving "group CBT." This may seem intimidating at first, but it has its own benefits.

Sometimes, when you see you are not alone, and there are many more like you have symptoms similar to you or even severe than yours, you tend to recover fast. Another example is Exposure and Response Prevention (ERP). Some other treatments include imaginal exposure, habit reversal training, etc.

Cognitive-Behavioral Therapy (CBT)

It is a psychotherapeutic treatment responsible for helping people to identify and then change the thought patterns that are disturbing, destructive, and impact their lives negatively.

The main focus of cognitive-behavioral therapy is to change your automatic negative thoughts, which can otherwise lead to anxiety, depression, and other emotional difficulties.

CBT identifies these thought patterns, challenges them, and finally changes them to rational and positive thoughts. There are several types of Cognitive-Behavioral therapy. They are:

- *Cognitive Therapy:* This is mainly responsible for identifying and bringing a change in the detrimental thought patterns, behaviors, and emotional responses.

- *Dialectical Behavioral Therapy:* This is mainly responsible for addressing the behaviors and thoughts and also for incorporating strategies like mindfulness and emotional regulation.

- *Multimodal Therapy:* This therapy suggests that the treatment of psychological issues must be done by addressing seven interconnected but different modalities. They are biological/drug considerations, interpersonal factors, cognition, imagery, sensation, behavior, and affect.

- *Rational Emotive Behavior Therapy (REBT):* This process is mainly responsible for the identification of all the irrational beliefs. It also challenges those beliefs and makes you recognize them and change them.

During the course of CBT, there are a number of challenges that people might face. They are:

- It can be really difficult to change. Some patients say that although they have identified some harmful and destructive thoughts, they find it very difficult (almost impossible) to change them.

- It is a very structured process. Changing the underlying unconscious resistances is not the focus of this procedure. It is suited for those patients who want to opt for a focused and target-based treatment approach.

- The treatment itself is not enough if you are not willing to change. If you want to make this work for you, you need to have a strong will to bring changes.

- You need to spend a lot of your efforts and time analyzing your feelings and thoughts. This self-analysis might seem difficult for a lot of people. But it is the only way of putting this process into effect and getting the most out of it.

Exposure and Response Prevention (ERP)

CBT deals with a lot of similar types of therapies. ERP is a specific type of CBT. The process has two parts: Exposure and Response Prevention.

The exposure part of this treatment mainly exposes you to the various situations, objects, images, and thoughts that are responsible for starting your obsessions or making you feel anxious.

The Response prevention part of this treatment mainly focuses on helping you to make a choice to not attempt some compulsive behaviors after your obsessions or anxieties got triggered—this process is performed by an experienced therapist in the beginning.

With time, you will be able to do ERP exercises on your own. If you are an OCD patient, you must have tried addressing the obsessive thoughts of yours to see if it helps.

ERP makes sure that when you address these thoughts, you also commit to yourself that you would do anything in your power to stop yourself from giving in to those compulsive behaviors. Once you stop those compulsive behaviors, you will notice a significant reduction in your anxiety levels.

Traditional psychotherapy or talk therapy helps the patient to gain insight into their actual problems. Psychotherapy can be very effective for the treatment of certain disorders, but it is not that effective in the case of OCD.

This is because in OCD, just having an insight is not enough. ERP helps you to identify, address, as well as commit to change.

Imaginal Exposure

Some people are not instantly ready to jump into real-world situations. Imaginal exposure helps to prepare them for getting ready for ERP. In this process, the therapist usually creates a scenario purposely for increasing the patient's anxiety levels.

For example, if someone is obsessed with walking in a particular manner, the therapist will show them a visual of someone walking in a divergent manner. This will trigger their anxiety, and the anxiety level will be noted down by the therapist.

After a certain amount of time, they will adapt to the anxiety and will get habituated. So, their anxiety will decrease over time. This will remove their strong repulsion towards that thing and will make them more open to trying out something new or challenging like the ERP.

Habit Reversal Training

This training process includes relaxation techniques, positive reinforcement, social support, competing for response introduction, and awareness training.

Awareness training involves identifying the habits and the sensations that occur in your body before engaging in a particular compulsive behavior. After you identify these sensations, you will be more aware of the changes that occur in your mind and body before the onset of compulsive behaviors.

Therefore, you will be able to control them or even stop them. Here comes the competing response. In this part, you and your therapist will work together to find an alternate response that you can do instead of your habit that won't be too noticeable.

For example, if you are someone with a vocal tic, you can just exercise the muscles around your mouth and cheeks and prevent yourself from giving in to your habit. If you have a tic of symmetrically touching things, you can try doing it with a different hand, or you can tightly hold it against your body to prevent the compulsion.

This process involves a lot of patience and determination. It is not possible to get results from this procedure for patients with severe OCD. It is a time-consuming process, and it requires family support in order to bring it to effect.

ACT (Acceptance and Commitment Therapy)

It is a new psychological therapy for treating people suffering from OCD. It has proved to be effective for treating OCD and some other anxiety disorders. The main philosophy of this treatment approach is that anxiety is a part of your life and your reaction to it is a real problem.

Other Treatments

Most of the patients suffering from OCD usually recover by the first-line treatments. But there are some patients who don't recover from any of these treatments. This condition is known as "treatment-resistant OCD." A very few people suffer from this.

The above-mentioned treatment options might be ineffective for about 25 to 40% of people. For them, there are some other treatment options that are not that common but are effective. These treatment approaches are:

Augmentation Therapy

This is the first thing that is tried on patients suffering from treatment-resistant OCD. In this process, a combination of drugs is used instead of using a single drug.

This is done in order to maximize the effect. A lot of people don't recover from a single drug but show a significant reduction in symptoms when a combination of drugs is used.

Repetitive Transcranial Magnetic Stimulation

In this therapy, specific regions of your brain are targeted using lasers. This process has been used since 1985. It is effective for relieving the intense feelings of depression, hopelessness, and sadness.

This process is FDA approved and can also, in some cases, be combined with antidepressants. This process is non-invasive, and the duration is somewhere around thirty to sixty minutes.

How Does RTMS Work?

You will have to sit down, and the doctor will place a specially designed electromagnetic coil near the brain area that is responsible for regulating moods. Magnetic pulses get generated by this coil to your brain.

You may feel a little tapping or knocking on your head, but that isn't painful at all. Electrical currents get generated in your nerve cells. After completion of this procedure, you can resume your regular activities.

These pulses are responsible for stimulating your brain cells in a way that your depression gets reduced. Some doctors can even position the coil in different places.

Side Effects

Some of the side effects of RTMS are:

- Tingling in the scalp, jaw, or face.

- Mild headaches.

- Lightheadedness.

Deep Brain Stimulation

Earlier electrodes were implanted in the anterior capsule of patients having treatment-resistant OCD. The results were promising. Almost three out of four people showed signs of remission.

Since then, emphasis has been increased on DBS research. With time, the target areas have shifted to the Ventral striatum or Ventral capsule (VC/VS), an overlapping part of the brain.

Almost 61.5% of patients suffering from treatment-resistant OCD displayed remission symptoms after undergoing DBS. SBS involves the opening of the skull, but no brain tissue gets damaged.

This process is approved by the FDA. The most important aspect of this process is positioning the electrodes and determining the amount of stimulation to be given to the patient.

It is a very crucial and risky treatment, so it is recommended that you receive DBS treatment from someone who has prior experience in this field.

How Does It Work?

The electrodes are placed at certain targeted areas of your brain. The pulse generators are positioned under your skin (usually under the collarbone).

The electrodes are then connected to these pulse generators with the help of wires. This pulse generator is also known as an implantable neurostimulator. This pulse generator consists of a microchip and battery.

The microchip is responsible for controlling the stimulation, whereas the battery provides the power. A small computer and a hand-held wand are used by the doctor for controlling the pulse generator through your skin.

The pulse generator of the pacemaker is similar to that of the DBS. The main difference is the positioning of the electrodes. A patient needs to continue DBS for a long amount of time, so it's better to get it done from some reliable place.

Electroconvulsive Therapy

This process is performed under general anesthesia. In this process, small amounts of electric currents are passed through your brain.

This is done to trigger a brief seizure. As a result, a lot of changes take place in your brain chemistry, thereby quickly reversing the OCD symptoms as well as certain other mental disorders.

The stigma attached to receiving ECT is totally based on some earlier incidents, where patients used to suffer fractured bones, memory loss, etc., for the use of high doses of electricity. But nowadays, ECTs are very safe and can be opted for getting better results in patients with treatment-resistant OCD. The doctors make sure that very little amounts of electric currents are passed and that too in a controlled environment, thereby ensuring utmost safety.

Risk Factors

- Although being widely used, it still has some risk factors. You may develop certain medical complications after receiving ECT. Medical procedures involving anesthesia can induce several medical complications. It causes an increase in blood pressure and heart rate. These may lead to severe heart problems. If you have a weak heart or some kind of heart disease, it is recommended that you don't go for this procedure.

- ECT can also have some physical side effects. You may experience muscle ache, jaw pain, headache, or nausea on the day you receive ECT. The side effects can be tackled by medications.

- A very rare side effect of this treatment is memory loss. Some people find difficulty in remembering what happened right before, or weeks before, or months before they received the treatment. In rare cases, patients even forget what happened a year before too. This condition is known as retrograde amnesia. In most cases, these problems vanish within a few weeks after the procedure.

- After finishing the procedure, you may feel a little confused for a little while. It may last for a few minutes to even a few hours. During this time, you might wonder where you are, and why you are there, etc. In worst-case scenarios, these confusions may last for several days. This side effect is observed mostly in older adults.

Brain Surgery

Bilateral Cingulotomy surgery is opted as a last resort by patients who don't show any signs of improvement from any other treatment approaches. It is a very risky treatment procedure for OCD and hence is opted by a very few numbers of treatment-resistant OCD patients.

It is also effective in treating chronic pain and depression. Mainly two parts of the brain are targeted by this surgery: the frontal lobes (responsible for regulating judgment, impulse control, reasoning, etc.) and the cingulate gyrus (responsible for regulating pain and emotions).

How Does It Work?

A gamma knife or an electrode is guided with the help of magnetic resonance imaging (MRI) to the cingulate gyrus. Then a half-inch burn or cut will be made by the surgeon for severing the circuit. You may take four days to recover from the surgery. Some side effects are vomiting, nausea, headaches, etc., for some days after the surgery.

In some cases, the surgery might also trigger seizures. Some patients experience memory lapses after the surgery, while some experience apathy. Although these side effects are rare, you still need to consider them before you go for this surgery.

Treatments for OCD usually involve visiting a medical professional and seeking help, but there are some other self-help strategies as well that you can use to bring the symptoms of OCD under control. Some of these are exercise, relaxation techniques, etc.

Chapter 6: Self-Assessment

The habit of assessing oneself is of prime importance to people of all ages and related to all kinds of work. If we have the ability to look at ourselves and all the actions that we undertake objectively, then it will be easier for us to find out the sectors where we need to improve and areas that need our attention immediately.

We will be able to freely learn from all the past mistakes we have made and also understand our growth over the years.

Though it is a practice that is easier said than done as becoming objective towards our own action is not easy a thing to do, yet, if a person gets in the habit of assessing one's own actions and decisions, they are sure to become much more confident and responsible human beings who are true to their word and also people who take responsibility of their actions.

That is why self-assessment has many advantages which should be known by all.

- Assessing one's own actions makes us more confident, and we become surer in our path of actions. What self-assessment does is eliminate all the uncertainties that we might be having as we get to ponder on our work more, and that reduces the work pressure we might be having because of failure and uncertainty.

- The second thing that will help a person who assesses their own work is to get done with the work in a much shorter time as they will have a much clearer vision and an idea regarding how things should be done.

- Self-assessment helps a person gain clarity regarding what they want and what they are not passionate about. Hence, they can make better choices for themselves without making mistakes. As they know where their talents lie, they can use that to their advantage.

- If a person assesses oneself then, he/she will be open to progressive criticism and changes as well. Assessing our own actions will show us in which departments we can bring a change in our lives to better our situation and grow more. It will help us break away from rigid superstitions and allow us to develop.

- Self-assessment helps us to train ourselves better and become better and a more polished version of ourselves. We tend to give up on things that hold us back, and we try to take such actions henceforth, which helps us strengthen our screens further and come out of the weaknesses we might have. We then become the best guide for ourselves as we start giving ourselves constructive criticisms, and we can tutor ourselves firmly.

- As we become a more confident version of ourselves, self-assessment also helps us flourish and work upon the strengths that we have, and we get more time to work upon them instead of wasting time on things that we don't have clarity for.

If a person is suffering from Obsessive Compulsive Disorder, then self-assessment can be of great help for a person to keep their OCD in check or even better to come out of it.

In most cases, a person is not aware of themselves having OCD as that becomes a part of their lives, and they tend to fail in understanding where they are going overboard with things.

That is the reason if they take a step back to assess their actions, it might become a bit easier for them to look into what they are doing wrong and as to how they can rectify those situations.

Any person who has OCD tends to obsess overdoing things in a particular way, and they tend to fuss a lot over getting things done in the way they prefer. So, in order for that to happen, they can even go to the extent of not accepting what others do, and that can cause a lot of misunderstandings and problems.

If one assesses their actions, they will clearly see these things, and it will then be easier for them to try and stop behaving in this way.

That is the reason we have prepared this MCQ test for everyone in general so that they can take the test for themselves and understand what situation they are currently in. anyone can take this test, and we hope that by giving honest answers to the given questions, it will be of great help to anyone reading this.

Before we start, we want to let everyone know that there are no right or wrong answers here and that it genuinely depends on however your personality is. So, be honest to yourself and choose the answer that comes to you naturally.

WORKBOOK EXERCISE

- Are you someone who is unable to stop yourself from thinking continuously about a particular thing?

  (a) YES (b) NO

- Do you at times feel ashamed of the thoughts you have and, as a result, fail to share them with others?

  (a) YES (b) NO

- Do you get unpleasant thoughts that you're unable to stop?

  (a) YES (b) NO

- Do you have the habit that you can't stop yourself from doing it even if you don't want to, like washing something again and again or repeatedly checking the locks?

  (a) YES (b) NO

- Do you have the habit of constantly repeating whatever you say, even if you have already gotten your answer on the first go?

  (a) YES (b) NO

- Are you someone who spends most of their time cleaning their surroundings and arranging and rearranging things in a particular way?

    (a) YES (b) NO

- Are you someone who feels anxious if the things in your surroundings are not the way you want them to be?

    (a) YES (b) NO

- Do you at times feel guilty because you act in this manner? Do you feel guilty because you are helpless in front of your habits?

    (a) YES (b) NO

- Are you someone who has this inherent fear in them of losing control over your thoughts and actions?

    (a) YES (b) NO

- Do you justify all the actions you take based on moral grounds?

    (a) YES (b) NO

We hope that this test has been helpful in letting you assess yourself, and if after this you feel that you need to take some constructive steps towards your betterment, we wish you all the best for that!

Chapter 7: Cognitive Behavioral Therapy or CBT for OCD

OCD is a serious issue and needs to be treated with utmost sincerity and care. There are a lot of treatment options available for the treatment of OCD.

Here, I am going to talk about a particular treatment approach, i.e., "Cognitive Behavioral Therapy" or "CBT."

What Is CBT?

CBT or Cognitive Behavioral Therapy is one type of psychotherapeutic treatment. This treatment allows people to identify disturbing or destructive thought patterns (these thoughts are detrimental to both your physical and mental health) and helps them to change them.

These negative thought patterns, if not changed, can have a bad impact on your emotions and behavior. Cognitive Behavior therapy is actually focused on changing your automatic destructive thoughts, which could otherwise contribute to worsening your anxiety, depression, and emotional difficulties.

Cognitive Behavior Therapy identifies, challenges, and replaces these negative thoughts with more realistic and objective thoughts.

Cognitive Behavioral Therapy Types

Cognitive Behavioral Therapy comprises a wide range of approaches and techniques for addressing behaviors, emotions, and thoughts. Starting from structured psychotherapies all the way to self-help materials, CBT has got everything covered. CBT has different types of treatment approaches. They are:

Cognitive Therapy: It falls under the larger group of Cognitive Behavioral therapies. Cognitive therapy is also a psychotherapeutic treatment approach developed by Aaron T. Beck, CT.

The duration of cognitive therapy is relatively short. Cognitive therapy is totally based on the theory that the way you feel about certain things is directly responsible for your emotional feelings.

Instead of focusing on past experiences, it is mainly focused on communication, behavior, and present thinking. This therapy is a goal-oriented program, and the goal is problem-solving.

Cognitive therapy has been found to be effective in treating personality problems, substance abuse, eating disorders, fears, panics, anxiety, depression, OCD, etc.

Cognitive therapy is also known as "Behavior therapy." This is because the main aim of this therapy is to affect the ways you think and the ways you act, i.e., your behavior.

- **Dialectical Behavior Therapy**: The process was developed by Dr. Marsha Linehan and her colleagues. It was developed when they found out that Cognitive Behavioral therapy as a whole is not being that effective for treating certain patients.

  For this reason, they added a few techniques, and then this process was developed for meeting all the unique needs of patients.

  It is a type of psychotherapy that is evidence-based. It came to action for treating borderline personality disorders. It teaches people to live in the moment.

  It is also associated with developing various healthy ways for improving your relationships with other people, regulating your emotions, and coping with stress.

  If you are someone who exhibits self-destructive behaviors and faces difficulty with emotional regulation, then DBT is the right treatment for you. It is also found to be effective in case of treating PTSD (Post Traumatic Stress Disorder).

- **Multimodal Therapy**: This method was devised by Arnold Lazarus. It is also a psychotherapeutic approach that is a type of cognitive-behavioral therapy.

  It is mainly based on the fact that human beings are biological creatures that interact, imagine, sense, act, feel, and think, and that the treatment approach needs to address all the modalities.

The assessment and treatment follow seven personality dimensions: biology/drugs, interpersonal relationships, cognition, imagery, sensation, affect, and behavior. Multimodal therapy is based on the fact that the therapist needs to address each and every modality in order to treat the various mental disorders. Every personality dimension gets affected differently in different human beings. The treatment should be done according to that; otherwise, it won't be effective.

- **Rational Emotive Behavior Therapy***:* REBT or Rational Emotive Behavior Therapy was introduced by Albert Ellis. This process helps you in identifying the negative thought patterns and the irrational beliefs that affect your behaviors and emotions.

    After you have successfully identified these, the therapist is going to help you in developing various strategies for replacing those with rational thought patterns.

    REBT is effective in treating people having: sleep problems, aggression, eating disorders, procrastination, overwhelming feelings (rage, guilt, or anger), phobias, addictive behaviors, anxiety, depression, etc.

Impact of Cognitive Behavioral Therapy

The backbone of the concept of CBT is based on the fact that your feelings and thoughts play a pivotal role in your behavior. For example, suppose a person who spends most of his time obsessing over the thoughts of air disasters, runway accidents, and plane crashes are likely to avoid air travel.

The main motive of Cognitive Behavioral Therapy is to make people understand that although they can't control everything that happens around them, they can have control over their reactions and thought processes about those things. In recent years, Cognitive Behavioral Therapy has gained a lot of popularity because of various reasons. Some of them are:

- Because of CBT, when people are finally able to identify their destructive thought patterns, they are starting to engage in healthy thinking patterns.

- If you are looking for a short-time treatment option that is highly effective, then Cognitive behavioral therapy is the right choice for you.

- If CBT works for you, then you won't be needing to take any other psychotropic medications.

- It has proved to be very effective in treating OCD and certain other mental-health-related disorders.

- It is comparatively cheaper than other costly therapies.

Benefits of Cognitive Behavioral Therapy

Cognitive Behavioral Therapy has a lot of benefits. They are:

- When people undergo CBT, they get a sense of hope that their condition is going to improve and that they won't have to spend their lives in misery. When a person suffers from OCD or other mental health disorders, they become really pessimistic when it comes to thoughts related to their future.

    They find it very difficult to look ahead to a time where they won't be bothered by this disorder. CBT changes this and gives them hope to have an optimistic view of their future life. It helps people to understand that sometimes people do behave in a way that is not "ideal," that your reactions might be inaccurate sometimes, and that you should not give up on yourself and should try to address these behaviors for changing them.

- Cognitive Behavioral Therapy is also responsible for boosting your self-esteem. People with OCD or other mental health disorders usually suffer from very low self-esteem. It is also a reason why they can't recover soon. This is because when you have low self-esteem, it caters to all the negative thought patterns that influence your behavior. Cognitive Behavioral Therapy is able to disrupt this particular pattern.

  As a result, you start developing confidence in yourself and also start believing in your abilities. When you finally understand your thoughts and how you control them, you can finally bring a change in your entire belief system.

- Cognitive Behavioral Therapy is also known for offering a sense of relaxation to the patients. CBT actually helps you to learn how to control your responses to your symptoms. CBT makes use of a lot of relaxation techniques for enabling you to develop calmer responses. As a result, you don't get triggered easily, and your symptoms get reduced eventually.

- Cognitive Behavioral Therapy allows you to develop rational thinking. The major benefit of this therapy is that it enables you to develop control over your thoughts. Sometimes cognitive distortions can automatically happen, but with time, you start questioning your disruptive thought patterns.

As a result, you become able to replace these negative thoughts and replace them with positive and rational ones. So, the negative thoughts will no longer be able to take control over you, and you will be able to rationally evaluate a situation and give a much appropriate response.

- CBT allows you to have mental support when you are recovering from the disorder. In the back of your head, you know that you have someone you can go to anytime to talk about your troubles and issues. The presence of a therapist is a huge mental support to the patients. When a patient knows that there is someone ready to help him whenever he needs it, the patient works harder to improve.

- People suffering from OCD or some other mental disorders tend to get triggered by a lot of things. This leads to anger, and anger leads to compulsive behaviors. Patients feel frustrated, ashamed, guilty for their obsessive thoughts, and they channelize their emotions to anger. Cognitive Behavioral Therapy focuses on addressing the underlying issues responsible for making these emotions so overwhelming. CBT helps you to learn different methods for controlling your emotional responses and assisting them in identifying the actual reasons behind your anger.

- Cognitive Behavioral Therapy is also known for improving your communication skills. When you are suffering from OCD, you also suffer from social anxiety, addiction, or depression. As a result, it becomes very hard for you to express yourself to others. This is because you are dealing with so much that you don't find the right words to make people understand your true feelings. At this point in time, it becomes very difficult to maintain personal or professional relationships. CBT allows you to speak your heart and mind out without getting angry, feeling shame, or feeling guilty.

- Cognitive Behavioral Therapy is known to improve your coping skills as well. A lot of mental disorders arise in the first place because of the lack of ability to cope with difficult situations like trauma, grief, confusion, aggression, frustration, etc. CBT gives you the strength to deal with these things. As a result, you stop bottling things up and start opening up more. This helps you to cope with difficult situations.

- Cognitive Behavioral Therapy also prevents patients from relapsing. Relapsing is common among patients who suffer from mental disorders. CBT provides various tools to the patients that help them to prevent these relapses.

- CBT allows patients to identify their underlying issues and how they can cope with them. So, patients have a clear understanding of what are the thoughts that they carefully need to avoid. When you avoid destructive thought patterns, you automatically prevent yourself from relapsing.

Pitfalls of Treating OCD Patients With CBT

People face several challenges during the course of undergoing Cognitive Behavioral Therapy.

Change Is Difficult

A lot of patients say that just identifying the harmful and irrational thoughts is not being of any help. It means that although they are aware of the negative thought patterns and the ways it affects their behavior and daily lives, they are still not being able to make any changes. Replacing these negative thoughts with positive and rational ones is not always possible, even if a person is fully aware of the disruptive thought patterns and the detrimental effects it has on life.

Cognitive Behavioral Therapy Is a Structured Process

CBT doesn't focus on changing the underlying unconscious resistances, like other treatment approaches. It is a much focused and structured process. The therapist plays an instructional role in this pr ocess. CBT looks at the bigger picture and aims at solving the root of all the problems, whereas other treatment approaches focus on reducing the symptoms. The fact that CBT is a much deeper thing makes it a very slow and structured process.

Patients Should Want to Change

Cognitive Behavioral Therapy demands determination. It is a process in which you won't be able to reach your end goals if you are not determined enough. If you are willing and ready to spend your efforts and time analyzing your thought patterns and feelings, this therapy can be effective. Analyzing your thoughts and feelings might seem difficult, but it is an amazing way by which you can learn how your innermost thoughts and feelings have a great impact on your day-to-day lives.

CBT Techniques Used for Treating OCD

Here are the main techniques of CBT that are implemented in the treatment of OCD.

ERP (Exposure and Response Prevention)

This process is mainly used in patients who have OCD. In this process, a therapist conducts several controlled ERP sessions with OCD patients.

While conducting the sessions, the therapist tactfully exposes these patients to several situations that can trigger their compulsions and obsessions. Initially, the patient might find it overwhelming, but gradually the patients find ways to deal with these.

Once the patient starts responding differently, the intensity of these obsessions and the frequency of these compulsive behaviors also get reduced. As a result, the OCD symptoms get milder, and sometimes, they even disappear. You need to explain to your therapist about your obsessive thoughts and compulsive behaviors in detail.

These must be ranked from the most triggering ones to the least bothering ones. The therapist usually begins with the least bothering ones and starts exposing you to those triggers. When you are able to resist these mild triggers, the therapist moves further to the more challenging ones.

The fact that your therapist is going to purposely expose you to things that make you feel uncomfortable might sound unfair to you. This is because, if you have OCD, you might have tried confronting these things several times, hoping that you would be able to overcome these, but failed. This makes you think that it is useless to go through that same torture all over again. But the thing is, ERP makes sure that you not only face these triggers but also commit to yourself to not give in. You need to make sure not to get engaged in any sort of compulsive behavior, irrespective of the triggers you are exposed to.

When you control yourself for a certain time and don't start behaving compulsively, your anxiety levels drop eventually with time. This is known as habituation, and this takes place when you manage to stay calm and prevent yourself from giving in to compulsive behaviors, even when you are exposed to your triggers for a long amount of time.

How Is ERP Different From Traditional Psychotherapy (Or Talk Therapy)?

In psychotherapy, the therapist usually talks to their patients to help them get a better insight and a clear understanding about what their problem is and what is the reason behind it. Psychotherapy can be very effective in treating some mental disorders, but in the case of OCD, it doesn't help much.

Psychotherapy can be a part of the treatment of an OCD patient, but it can't be the only treatment. It can't substitute ERP when it comes to treating an OCD patient.

Exposure Ritual Prevention and Awareness Exercises

It's important to understand how exposure ritual prevention and awareness (ERPA) exercises affect symptoms. So let's look at the series of events that occur during a cycle of obsessive-compulsive disorder, commonly referred to as an OCD spike.

First, there is a trigger; something noticed in your physical, social, or mental world. Second, it immediately activates an obsession - painful thoughts, feelings, or impulses. Almost at the same time, you experience fear, guilt, apprehension, fear, anger, or any number and combination of distressing emotions.

These three events - exposure to a trigger, activation of an obsession, and feelings of distress - are perceived as a single event together. Hence, the terms "trigger," "obsession," and "distress" are used interchangeably to refer to this seemingly unique event - the climax.

Your natural reaction is to turn it off asap. Eventually, through trial and error, you will find that by repeating certain actions and/or certain mental gyrations you can get temporary relief until the next obsession occurs.

ERPA exercises deal with each of these events. First, you choose a trigger for a particular combination of obsession and compulsion and then practice exposing yourself to that trigger. During exposure, the next step is to refrain from rituals and instead practice awareness of the distress.

If this is done successfully, the distress will go away. Because the obsessions that once caused terrible fear no longer have that power, they become meaningless, which makes them more intrusive and repetitive. Since there are no obsessions, no compulsions are required.

WORKBOOK EXERCISE

To prepare for an exposure exercise, do the following:

Choose a trigger, a combination of obsession and compulsion to eliminate.

Practice exposure by bringing on an obsession with reality and imagination.

Practice ritual prevention by avoiding compulsions and fear blocking behaviours.

Practice acceptance; fully experience the thoughts, images, impulses, emotions and physical sensations that are triggered.

Write down your thoughts in detail.

Selecting an Obsessive-Compulsive Combination for Elimination

The best combination of obsession and compulsion to focus on is typically the less stressful combination of obsession and compulsion. Even if you are trying to get rid of the most annoying symptoms, it is best to start with one that offers the best chances of success. Because nothing works like success.

Don't worry; we'll cover all your triggers eventually. As you know, there is a certain stress associated with the exercises you want to perform. So start with the easiest to minimise the burden.

Write your most stressful combination of obsession and compulsion.

_____
_____
_____
_____
_____
_____
_____

Write your least stressful combination of obsession and compulsion.

_____
_____
_____
_____
_____
_____
_____

Exposure, Bringing on the Obsessions

Exposure involves contact with triggers of obsessions in reality, which are in the outer, physical and social world, or in imaginary situations, which are in the inner, mental world, because fear is the problem and fear is the solution. I realize that the idea of coping with fear is rather frightening, but necessary.

On a case-by-case basis, patients indicated that once they began to deal with anxiety, they did not find it as painful as expected. Most important, they discover that the exposure works. Obsessions no longer trigger fear and become simple "thoughts". Because they are neutral and have no emotional impact, they are irrelevant and gradually disappear.

Write down what triggers you.

_____
_____
_____
_____
_____
_____
_____
_____
_____
_____
_____
_____
_____
_____
_____
_____
_____
_____

Shaping

Remember that exposure exercises are carried out more gradually moving towards a goal slowly. This type of progressive advancement is called shaping.

Begin with a situation that causes minimal stress and stay with it until you have little to no response. Only then face another situation, only a bit harder than the first, and stay with it until the distress goes away.

This process will go on until you have been completely exposed to all your obsessions, including what you found most frightening in the beginning.

When you get there, you will be desensitized from previous exposure exercises, so the last step will not be harder than the first. This process of taking small actions to achieve a target is an important part of the recovery process.

For exposure to eliminate fear, 2 conditions are necessary. Firstly, rituals and other measures to avoid exposure should be avoided. The use of fake fear blockers is discussed in detail in the next section.

The second condition is the requirement for prolonged exposure. Exposure sessions should be sufficiently long for you to notice a significant decrease in your distress during exposure.

This means your sessions can last an hour or more. What people usually feel during their sessions is a gradual increase in stress that becomes stable after a few minutes. Then it starts to sink. In this phase, you are going to experience the benefits of exercise.

No matter what the trigger, it loses its power to induce fear. During the following exposure sessions, you will see that fear is weak at first and disappears faster until you finally feel little or no distress. You will have neutralized the trigger and learned that exposure alone will free you from anxiety without resorting to the use of faulty fear blockers.

Keep your exposure sessions not more than 90 minutes by choosing triggers which are in the easy to moderate difficulty level.

Exposure can be mentally and emotionally stressful so you don't want to create unnecessary trouble by overdoing it. If you underestimate the power of a trigger and find it takes more than 90 minutes for the stress to wear off, stop working on it and replace it with an easier exercise.

You may return to what you underestimated after the simple exercises desensitize you. As stated above, exposure exercises may be in reality or in the imagination. Reality exposures focus on eliminating obsessions triggered by real situations, your physical and social environment. These exposure activities call for being physically involved in situations that trigger obsessions.

Exposures in the imagination aim at eliminating obsessions triggered by thoughts and images of imaginary future events which are impossible and unlikely. Such exposures, which only exist in your head, require contact with imagined triggers. One of the best ways to get the imagination going is to write down the contents of your obsessions and audio tape that scenario and listen to it for as long as it takes to feel some relief. You can also practice exposing yourself to this scenario by rewriting and re-reading it for a prolonged period of time until you feel that your stress is dissipating.

For either type of exposure exercise, it is of the utmost importance that you do not stop while your anxiety grows. This will avoid desensitization and may even raise your awareness of the situation you are attempting to neutralize.

With this in mind, plan your exposure sessions for times when you have plenty of time to finish and know you won't be interrupted or distracted. To achieve better results, practice daily, including weekends and holidays. A momentum develops which makes practice easier with faster results. I also suggest doing the exercises at the beginning of the day. This will reduce your risk of pushing them away.

EXPOSURE EXERCISE

Write rituals and other measures that you use to avoid exposure.

_____
_____
_____
_____
_____
_____
_____
_____
_____
_____

Ritual Prevention Refraining from False Fear-Blocking Behavior

A fake fear blocker is any action or thought that immediately follows an obsession that lessens fear. I use the term "fake" because reduced fear is temporary and reverts to the next obsession. Its biggest harm is to block the exposure, thereby preventing recovery.

The most common false fear blockers are physical and mental compulsions, distraction, avoidance, and reassurance seeking. Physical and mental compulsions are voluntary acts which are within your control. Just as you can control how your muscles move, you can also control the performance of physical rituals.

The same applies to mental rituals; these are intentional words you say to yourself and images you produce intentionally. The question is not "Can I prevent rituals?" but: "Am I prepared to prevent them?" If you want to defeat OCD the answer must be "yes". The price you pay to drop them - a slight short-term fear - is worth the long-term advantages of not having Obsessive Compulsive Disorder.

The old saying "It's easier than you think" has been held to be true by all brave people who have given up rituals and overcome their suffering. You can become one of them. Keep in mind that by designing your exposures, you can control your anxiety levels, making it easier to complete the rituals. Distraction is likely one of the first false fear blockers people deal with obsessions.

While trying to focus on something else, they hope to ignore the obsessions related to their anxiety and distress. Being actually aware of what you are doing, being constantly busy and moving are opportunities for those who have a more energetic tendency to compete with repetitive intrusive thoughts and images. Listening to music, talking constantly and without thinking is used by others who attempt to mitigate the effects of obsessions.

Those who tend to worry may even concentrate on boring daily problems to get their obsessions out of their mind. The most drastic and downright dangerous distraction is self-inflicted injuries, often to the head, as if casting out demons, atoning for guilt, or trading physical pain of emotional anguish.

Distractions, like their cousins who block fear, compulsions, provide only short-term, often unpredictable relief from the distress of the inevitable recurring obsessions. Distractions need to be let go of in order for the real fear blocker to fail - exposure. Avoidance, as you now know, is the opposite of exposure and stands in the way of recovery.

Before you had this knowledge, however, you did what came naturally and you remained away from the triggers which activated irrational images and thought impulses. You must now take the path of recovery that follows fear. If you stray from it and wander into the wasteland of avoidance, your journey will be endless. Avoided situations can be your ally when you realize that they are actually triggers of your obsessions and, as such, targets of desensitization. When they have been neutralized and you can approach them with ease, you have proven the ultimate proof of successful treatment.

Reasoning is probably the most commonly used fear blocker, although most of the time the person realizes his or her fears are unreasonable. However, during severe OCD spikes, that understanding weakens and doubts arise that the feared thoughts may be real. For example, can thoughts really mean, "I have a major character flaw or I'm insane?" Like nature abhors a vacuum, humans hate uncertainty.

We deal with it by rationalizing, analysing, intellectualizing, theorizing and applying all kinds of mind manipulations in order to obtain certainty. This happens to OCD when faulty fear blockers to think about things and question irrational thoughts are involved. As you are well aware, these aid efforts are in vain.

We have little direct control over our emotional reactions. Our rational control of fear is weak; but fear can easily divert rational control by doing it routinely in OCD. Indeed, the links between emotional systems in the brain and rational systems are stronger than the links between rational systems and emotional systems (LeDoux, 1996).

Philosophers, poets, and other great people have expressed this understanding over the centuries and joining them today are neuroscientists sharing discoveries about how the brain works. Keep in mind with fear that what you think will not help you, but what you do will.

Assurance is one of the strongest and unrecognized of these fear and recovery blockers. This is a form of compulsion that I have observed in more than 90% of the people I have worked with. As many people compulsively seek to reassure themselves in order to calm their OCD and anxiety, this deserves special attention. People with obsessive-compulsive disorder worry about their obsessions coming true.

To ease this distress, they repeatedly ask other people, usually family members or close friends, to reassure them that their fears will not materialize. As obsessions are always unrealistic, family members or friends (and even therapists) tell them that there is nothing to be afraid of, nothing bad will happen.

For example, it is very common for people who are afraid of being irresponsible or reckless to seek assurance that they are not. Usually they get the reassurance they want and temporary relief, but like other compulsions, reassurance block recovery. This is the first paradox.

Reassurance is not good - it's bad. However, the short-term relief is so gratifying that the person is constantly in search of more, which is the second paradox. The more we are reassured, the more we want to be reassured. Trying to satisfy that demand is the same as trying to fill a bottomless well.

The constant demands for comfort can not only hamper recovery, but also become imposing demands that lead to interpersonal conflict. In one case, a woman's husband's inquiry became so intense and frequent, that she moved out and rented her own apartment. Then her husband took part in an intensive treatment program that helped both and the reassurance stopped.

That's an example of paradox number three. Once reassurance is removed, the person no longer finds the desire for it, accompanied by a decrease in obsessions and other compulsions. So how should you handle your desire to ask to be reassured?

First, stop asking for reassurance. Determine the questions you ask most often and do not ask them. Try to avoid subtle, indirect ways of reassuring yourself. These may be unknown to the researchers, but are knowingly practiced by you. For example, one client I worked with would abruptly stop doing whatever she was doing sit down and space out. Her husband learned that these behaviours indicated that she was caught in obsessions, and they became a nonverbal request to reassure that he would give immediately.

It was his cue to tell her not to worry, that her fears were irrational, that it was just her obsessive-compulsive disorder. In addition to responding to obvious requests, subtle, indirect also need to be stopped.

Second, educate your significant others about the negative effects of reassurance. Have them read this passage. Explain that reassurance is bad for recovery.

Third, create a gentle refusal statement. At first, you are likely to continue to seek reassurance, even if you are trying to get away from it. Therefore, the people who normally reassure you must work with you to create an acceptable way to say no. One way to do that is to say, "I think you're seeking reassurance. Remember, reassurance is not helpful. It is dangerous.

Therefore, I will not reply. " However, if this doesn't work, it's possible that the agreed upon statement itself has become reassuring or that you believe that nothing bad will happen because the reassurer would warn you. In this case, the best way to stop it is for the parties to stop speaking entirely of OCD.

WORKBOOK EXERCISE

Write the questions you ask most often for reassurance.

_____
_____
_____
_____
_____
_____
_____
_____
_____
_____
_____
_____
_____
_____
_____
_____
_____
_____
_____
_____
_____
_____
_____
_____

Awareness

I think everyone has heard you have to deal with your fears in order to overcome them. It's easy to say, but hard to do. Our instinctive response to the threat is fight or flight. This reaction has a survival value to face the actual dangers, but not the false dangers you fear in OCD. Surviving for you means overcoming OCD, which requires feeling fear, holding on to it, getting involved and overcoming it.

Reading it can arouse anticipatory fears. Remember, however, that you can manage your anxiety levels by gradually approaching the triggers so that you are experiencing only mild to moderate anxiety. Upon contact, you can notice that anxiety gradually increases, then stabilizes, and after some time, it decreases.

During this last phase, you experience the benefits of the treatment. You are desensitized. When confronted with fear, your job is to pay attention to your uncomfortable thoughts, emotions and physical sensations. Dwell on the creepy thoughts and pictures. Do the opposite of what you have done and embrace the fears as best you can. Imagine the dreaded future events.

Tell yourself, "So be it." Focus on the prospect of living in a world of uncertainty, never knowing if and when something bad will happen, never getting over the state of fear, and so on. Keep thinking about your thoughts and throwing images to intentionally create fear. That's how you use fear to fight fear.

You cannot overcome fear by trying to get around it, but only by going through it. Be truly conscious of your emotions. Also, be mindful of your body's physical reactions. Where do you feel the fear inside you? If your heart beats faster, pay attention.

If you experience muscle tension, concentrate on it. If you breathe faster and harder, notice it. Does your stomach and chest feel tight? Are you feeling hot? Are you sweating? If the answer is yes, it means you are on the right track because you experience fear and let it wear out. By pursuing fear, you destroy it. All those terrible feelings are for the good.

You will know for yourself, after many exposures the fear will not exist anymore. You cannot invoke it even if you try to. However, you may be preoccupied with the fact that obsessions will become stronger if you abandon your efforts to stop blocking them, or if you do them deliberately. Or perhaps you're afraid that what you fear might happen. Paradoxically, no such results occur.

Instead, just the opposite happens; you will recover after retraining your brain's fear system to stop making false alarms about harmless events.

You will be desensitized to the previous fear triggers and see them as they truly are - harmless thoughts and images that are simply part of the normal flow of your stream of consciousness. In other words, OCD is erased when undesirable pictures and thought impulses are confronted and embraced.

You may ask, "If exposure to fear is only needed to overcome Obsessive-Compulsive Disorder, why hasn't this already happened?" I've had these obsessions for many years and they keep coming back. The answer is that you used futile fear blockers to eliminate the distress from obsessions.

This means that your fear exposures have not been long enough for it to fall naturally, which it will simply be due to your feeling. You will fully understand the truth on this subject after completing your first exposure exercise.

WORKBOOK EXERCISE

Write down your fears.

Write down your emotional and physical reaction to those thoughts.

The above exercises may sound intimidating. However, keep in mind the advantages they offer.

1. Changes in emotions as a result of lower anxiety or no anxiety.

2. Enable rational thoughts to replace irrational thoughts.

3. Ability to maintain a job, volunteer, or pursue educational or training goals.

4. Engage in ordinary interests and routines.

5. Enjoyment of satisfying family and social activities and relationships. Good luck. You've got the power!

Cognitive Therapy

As discussed earlier, it is focused on identifying and modifying the thought patterns that are responsible for causing negative behaviors, distress, or anxiety. Cognitive therapy helps you to understand that your brain is sending faulty messages. Cognitive therapy allows you to understand these faulty messages and enables you to respond in a different way, thus allowing you to confront these obsessions.

Cognitive therapy is conducted with a few outpatient sessions and some homework that patients need to complete between the therapy sessions. If you have extreme OCD, then you might need frequent therapy sessions with your therapist.

You might feel that this treatment is useless as you have tried to resist compulsions earlier on your own. But it can be effective when you are in good hands. A good therapist can actually make it work for you. It has been found to be very effective in several studies. All you need to do is be a little willing to bring change.

Metacognitive Therapy

Metacognitive therapy helps OCD patients to emotionally detach themselves from the obsessions. It enables them to observe these obsessions without judging. As a result, they are able to ignore harmful and intrusive thoughts. It changes your perception regarding the significance of the intrusive thoughts and the need to give a reaction to these thoughts.

Strategies of Cognitive Behavioural Therapy for Treating OCD

Certain feelings or thoughts force people to reinforce faulty beliefs. This results in a problematic behavioral pattern having adverse effects on academics, work, romantic relationships, family, etc. The strategies that are used in CBT are as follows:

Identifying Negative Thoughts

In order to treat disruptive thinking patterns, the most important thing that needs to be done at first is to identify all the negative thought patterns that are affecting your feelings and behaviors. The therapist talks with you and runs several assessments for identifying the negative thought patterns.

Practicing New Skills

Starting to practice new skills is very important so that they can be implemented in real-life situations for getting a better outcome. For example, if an OCD patient has a tendency to repeat a certain thing, then he or she might start practicing how to avoid it or find a different thing to do instead of that.

It enables people to develop new coping mechanisms so that they can have control over their emotions and actions while being in a social situation. It helps you to stay unbothered from all the possible triggers and prevents you from relapsing.

Setting Goals

A very important part of recovering from mental disorders is goal setting. It helps you in making changes for improving your life and health. The therapist will teach you how you can identify your goals, how can you distinguish between long-term goals and short-term goals, how can you set goals (time-based, relevant, attainable, measurable, specific), and how can you start focusing on the process as well instead of just focusing on the end result.

Problem-Solving

It is very important to learn problem-solving skills. It helps you in identifying and solving the problems that arise from stressful situations. Problem-solving skills help you in reducing the negative impacts of mental illnesses.

Problem-solving usually consists of five steps: identification of the problem, finding a few possible solutions of each problem, evaluation of the weaknesses and strengths of all the possible solutions, Selection of a possible solution, and its implementation.

Gradual Progress

Cognitive Behavioral Therapy is a gradual process. It takes time to implement behavioral changes. CBT helps you to take incremental steps slowly towards attaining a certain behavioral change.

For example, if someone is having obsessive thoughts over doing something wrong in a social situation, he or she might start imagining themselves in a social situation. After successful completion of this step, he or she can further move to imagine a conversation, and so on. When you are working progressively towards a particular goal, it seems that the process is easy and effective in helping you achieve your end goals.

Chapter 8: Imaginal Exposure Therapy

A huge number of therapies, especially behavioral therapies, are there that are helpful in treating OCD or obsessive-compulsive disorder. It is true that the techniques or procedures of every single behavioral therapy are different from the others. But, the therapies do have one thing in common.

Usually, their main aim is to expose the individual having OCD to such things which he/she fears the most, such as a disturbing thoughts. Though behavior therapies like imaginal exposure therapy prove to be quite effective, yet about two-thirds of people who have mental condition like OCD complete the entire treatment.

The remaining fraction of patients step back because they are afraid of experiencing severe distress accompanied by exposure exercise. A lot of patients do exist who are unable to thoroughly understand the logic or principle behind the treatments based on therapy.

Thus, such individuals do face a bit of difficulty adhering to the progress of such treatments when things begin to get tough. Hence, it is better to understand each and every part of imaginal exposure therapy as it will assist in improving the chances of a better success rate.

Exposure therapy has been developed to assist people in confronting their personal fears. If an individual is afraid of something, then he/she tries to avoid the activities, situations, or objects that he/she fears. Avoiding such things may help in decreasing the frightening feelings for the short term, but situations may become worse in the long term.

It is in these situations that a proficient psychologist comes to the rescue. They recommend the appropriate version of exposure therapy to the patient for breaking the patterns of fear and avoidance. In exposure therapies, the medical professional helps in creating a safe and secure environment for exposing the patients to those things that they usually tend to avoid.

As the person is exposed to his/her feared activities or objects and that too in an extremely safe environment, his/her fear and avoidance also get reduced gradually. It does not matter what form of OCD you are struggling with; imaginal exposure therapy is an essential technique that needs to be added to the toolkit. Here you will get to know almost everything about imaginal exposure therapy for treating obsessive-compulsive disorder.

What Is Imaginal Exposure Therapy?

First of all, you need to know one fact about imaginal exposure therapy is that it has proved to be one of the best and the most advantageous treatment tools for those people who are struggling with obsessive-compulsive disorder as well as associated anxiety disorders. But, for understanding the technique of imaginal exposure therapy in the best possible way, it is necessary to have a basic idea of ERP or exposure and response prevention.

Exposure and response prevention is one particular form of CBT or cognitive behavioral therapy. A huge number of researchers have repeatedly and consistently found it to be the best and efficient treatment for obsessive-compulsive disorder. The primary rule of ERP is exposing an individual repeatedly to their fear and that too without performing any actions related to compulsive anxiety reduction. By doing so, the person will start becoming less frightened when they face situations that provoke anxiety.

This particular procedure is referred to as habituation. It is simply a special or ornamental way of revealing the fact that people suffering from mental condition or other anxiety disorders tend to get less scared of certain things just because they confront such things repeatedly.

If someone is scared of touching doorknobs as he/she thinks that by doing so, they may catch any type of communicable disease, then a basic ERP interference is making them touch knobs repeatedly and not letting them wash hands afterward. In the same manner, if you think negatively about your house catching fire and thus check the stove knobs repeatedly, then ERP would let you use the stove but not allow you to check the knobs once you are done using the stove. The focus or main aim of ERP is to alter the different types of fear response just by confronting the affected person's behaviors.

A lot of people suffering from OCD struggle more with unwanted mental images and distressing thoughts and less with noticeable outwardly compulsive behaviors. This matter is true for people having variants of obsessive-compulsive disorder. It is often referred to as Pure O or Pure obsessional OCD. Some of the forms of OCD in this category include HOCD, Harm OCD, Scrupulosity, and ROCD.

For people who are suffering from any of these types of OCD, imaginal exposure therapy acts to be the most powerful in such cases. In imaginal exposure therapy, the medical professionals will assist you in using your own imaginations for confronting any type of feared thoughts and consequences directly.

The uncomplicated and transparent concept behind imaginal exposure therapy for treating OCD is penning down as well as reading very short stories that are related to the affected person's obsessive thoughts. But, such stories are not like the other stories that people love to read as they are something more than that.

The reason behind this is that those stories are related to the patient's horrifying thoughts. The darkest and deepest OCD thoughts of the sufferer are dragged to the most unfavorable outcome. But, you might be shocked to know that a maximum number of individuals who are suffering from OCD are not that much interested in the concept of writing down stories that are related to their worst possible scenario.

A very usual fact about imaginal exposure therapy for treating OCD is that a lot of patients either begin shedding tears or quit the therapy when the concept of reading and writing stories related to their fears is brought to light for the first time. Thus, stories of imaginal exposure should be used only after an individual gets a feeling that he/she is ready to confront his/her scariest thoughts. One thing that is very much essential for this therapy is that the client or patient must feel adequately safe with the procedure of exposure. The individual with OCD must also feel safe for going to any place that he/she thinks is unsafe.

Imaginal exposure therapy's goal is to let the affected person experience a feeling of anxiety without turning or moving away from the scenario, which means not reassuring, neutralizing, undoing, or distracting. In exposures like this, an individual who is going through the therapy is instructed to face the situation or fear mentally by visualizing or imagining it in his/her mind. For example – if a person is scared of very crowded places, that is, if he/she is suffering from agoraphobia, then they may visualize standing or visiting a busy and congested shopping mall.

Though there are various reasons for pursuing imaginal exposure therapy, yet the main reason is that this therapy permits the affected individual to be exposed effectively to certain thoughts that are obsessional. It is effective as such thoughts may not possess any sort of noticeable compulsions. Apart from that, a few more reasons do exist for which this particular therapy may prove to be one of the most efficient approaches to exposure. Have a look at the reasons –

- Certain thoughts are there that cannot be executed because of ethical and legal reasons. Just like, you cannot appoint someone for slaying someone or for molesting a small kid.

- It is not always easy to create standard behavioral exposure for certain thoughts. Suppose a person having an existential obsessive-compulsive disorder is scared of non-existence, then in such situations forming behavioral exposures replicating the non-existing is practically impossible or absurd.

- Some people become excessively anxious if provoked by some particular thoughts. Many individuals having OCD are so much affected with tension or uneasiness regarding a specific thing, situation, or event that penning down short stories based on the things that they are afraid of may prove to be a nice transitional move that will assist them in confronting their fear more straightforwardly.

No matter what the actual reason is, the technique of imaginal exposure therapy may possess an excellent effect on people with OCD, only when they get ready for both writing and utilizing imaginal exposures.

Facts About Writing Stories of Imaginal Exposure

First of all, such stories are penned down with the active participation of the person with OCD, and the stories are totally based upon their real obsessions. In order to be highly effective, the stories of imaginal exposure therapy need to have a total number of six particular and distinct features. The presence of those characteristics guarantees to provide the best impact. Thus, have a look at the specific characteristics.

- It would be best to keep in mind that you have to write the stories in the present tense. You must not write such as the event occurred a year before. It is better to avoid the past tense and try writing like the things or events are occurring in the present time. You may also portray your story as if the consequence of any event is happening now.

- Another essential feature of such stories is that they must be written by using the first person. Instead of writing 'she pushed her boyfriend into the lake,' you need to write 'It is I who pushed my boyfriend into the lake.' You must remember one thing that the imaginative stories written by you are not at all about any other third person. The stories are only about 'you.

- The stories must be realistic by nature. You need to imagine only to that extent that is convincing or trustworthy to you at first.

- The next feature about imaginal exposure therapy stories is that the writer or the sufferer needs to keep the stories real. In other words, if you are finding something to be annoying or irritating at present, then you need to write a story about that actual thought. If you find out that you are not getting bothered by that thought, then it is better not to spend your valuable time just by writing about that.

- The stories of imaginal exposure need to be dragged to the extreme point. It will serve the best purpose if the stories are made as bad as possible, just like the participant's personal nightmare. The extreme points may be living in hell forever, sentenced to death for murdering, or spending the remaining days of your life with guilt in your mind that your own daughter has been sexually molested by you.

- The next important characteristic of an imaginal exposure story is that the writer must write it in a brief manner and not keep a moderate tone. One needs to keep one thing in mind that this phase of the therapy is not at all similar to any creative writing classes. Suppose you are obsessed with hurting or injuring someone, then your short story needs to be about acting that thought of yours as well as the dangerous outcome, where you need to pay for your deed.

The stories that you need to write as a part of this therapy should be comparatively shorter than any other creative or imaginative story. They must not be more than a half to three-fourth page. There is no necessity of including any sort of metaphors and attractive adjectives in your story. Your focus must be to adhere to the main content with its inhuman or harsh glory. In simple words, your imaginative story should be very much powerful, be it a story of a single sentence or half a page.

Now, after the person with OCD has completed writing his/her story, he/she needs to read it out repeatedly and that too very loudly. A maximum number of exposure therapists recommend their clients that they should read their stories at least thirty times a day. Now, you might be thinking about how that is possible as everyone leads a busy life.

Well, you need not worry at all as this goal of reading thirty times can be achieved by following this simple step – read your story ten times before you start working, another ten times during your lunch hour, and the remaining ten times once you are done with your work. No matter how hectic your schedule is, while reading, you should maintain a steady pace and avoid speedy reading.

The main aim is to feel the story's full impact, and so therapists suggest not reading it quickly. In order to get the entire benefit of imaginal exposure therapy, it is necessary to go through the exposure stories a lot of times. Only then will you be able to observe significant and desired results.

There is another effective alternative to this procedure of reading your story on a daily basis. If you find that you are somehow unable to read so many times because of your extremely busy lifestyle, then you may better record your short story so that you may hear it attentively as many times as possible.

Recording your story is a nice option as you will be able to listen to the recorded audio while traveling to work as well as at the time of returning home. In this way, you will be able to utilize your time in a systematic manner. Read and, at times, listen to the story until you get a feeling that it is less threatening than before, or until it turns to be an extremely boring story that you don't feel like reading anymore. In this particular case, boredom is actually good.

In many cases, it might happen that a specific story does not cause anxiety anymore, but the obsession still remains the same. Then, in such situations, the person suffering from OCD needs to pen down another new story, and that has to be worse than the previous one. Just like a person needs to adapt his/her behavioral exposures according to the altering compulsions, in a similar manner, it is also necessary to readjust imaginal exposures for obsessions that gradually change.

If you suddenly notice that you are confronting an obsession that is absolutely new, then the next process of imaginal exposure therapy is to write a story that is brand new, and it also has to provoke your anxiety uniformly. The faster you confront your new obsession, the less will it get rooted firmly in your brain.

While pursuing the therapy for dealing with OCD as well as afterward, you will be able to benefit a lot if you pen down numerous exposure stories that threaten the various obsessions that you possess. Experienced exposure therapists always keep on suggesting that people who are suffering from obsessive-compulsive disorder must remain proactive for their own benefit.

A lot of you may think that imaginal exposure therapy is scary or dark by nature. But, it is not true at all. In the beginning, you may find it to be a bit difficult or feel uneasy while exposing your fearful imaginations.

But, gradually, you will realize the effectiveness of this particular therapy for treating OCD.

By following the technique of confronting your scary thoughts, with the passage of time, you will learn that your thoughts are not that much frightening as you believed them to be. Moreover, an individual with OCD is not performing the activities that he/she is afraid of.

Another aim of this therapy is to provide permission to yourself for experiencing thoughts that are unwanted. By doing so, you will gradually understand that those undesired and scary thoughts are not at all worthy of the excessive attention as well as anxiety that you once gave them. With steady effort or attempt, you will observe that the symptoms of OCD are decreasing gradually with each passing day.

The response of imaginal exposure therapy is not the same for every person; it varies from one person to the other. The variation in response occurs due to several factors. They are:

- A person's eagerness in writing the exposure stories reflecting his/her deepest and darkest fears.

- Analyzing the severity of the symptoms that are obsessional by nature.

- The sufferer's assurance or obligation that he/she will read the stories consistently and repeatedly, without skipping for even a day.

Thus, people who are struggling a lot with an obsessive-compulsive disorder or any other related disorder can challenge their anxiety by practicing this therapy. Just like any other exercise, imaginal exposure therapy does work for dealing with people suffering from OCD, and the best result is only produced if they follow the techniques till the end.

WORKBOOK EXERCISE

Write the story related to your obsessive thoughts.

Chapter 9: ACT and Mindfulness

Every individual is different with varying degrees of difficulty. It is therefore impossible for counselors and psychologists to come up with a single solution that will be one-type-fits-all. The introduction of lesser practiced solutions can prove to be fruitful as some OCD patients may respond well and quickly to these methods.

OCD or Obsessive-Compulsive Disorder, as you already know, involves the completion of compulsions or stereotypical repetitive behaviors depending on the obsessions of the patient. Obsessions here imply the patient's encounter with his or her unwanted and recurrent intrusive thoughts. These symptoms may worsen in cases where the person facing them is repetitively trying to suppress them or deny those thoughts.

The two methods we are going to discuss today - Mindfulness and ACT (Acceptance and Commitment Therapy and Mindfulness) - helps an OCD patient by working on these areas and help them with their condition by giving them a new way of looking and facing these intrusive thoughts.

Mindfulness

An OCD patient seeking therapy or treatment must have come across the term "mindfulness" at least once during their journey. Mindfulness is simply trying to stay in the present moment and not obsessing over any other futuristic thoughts. As easy as it may sound, it is not that easy for someone with Obsessive-Compulsive Disorder.

The person has repetitive, intrusive thoughts throughout their day that causes them to constantly worry or obsess over things. Several techniques teach a person with the disorder to use distractions to distance themselves from their intrusive thoughts or ways of neutralizing their fears that are inflicted through a sudden burst of their thoughts.

However, mindfulness is a little different or rather conflicting from these techniques as instead of telling the patient ways of running away from the thoughts or suppressing or hiding them, it asks the patient to acknowledge them.

Even people without OCD have a random burst of thoughts that are unrealistic and make them feel threatened, just like people with OCD. Then how are the two groups of people different? The other group of people simply accepts the thought as just another thought, whereas OCD patients have a difficult time acknowledging the fact that these are just thoughts in their head.

To simply say, OCD patients are trapped inside their inner thoughts and fail to accept reality for what it is. They consider these inner experiences as warning signs or consider them as alarms to danger. Some even take these thoughts to be true to such an extent that they start considering them as a potential threat to them.

The problem thus lies in not being able to distinguish these inner experiences from reality. Mindfulness which simply preaches to remain in the present moment, allows or shows ways of accepting these experiences for what they are - mere thoughts cooked up by their creative minds. This technique, therefore, asks the patient to incorporate the therapeutic concept of "it is just a thought."

Based on the approach, mindfulness therapy is considered similar to the ERP (exposure with response prevention) treatment as this technique too asks the individual to acknowledge the thoughts and to be aware of what triggers them. After acknowledging their trigger factor, they are then asked to work on the ability to not respond to these triggers.

However, mindfulness is slightly different as it asks the patient to accept the inner experiences but in a non-judgmental way. It also asks the patient to stay in the moment and feel all the thoughts, even though they might be extremely painful or frightening, and then do nothing about it. Feel and accept the thoughts and experiences as simple thoughts that are unreal, thus making the therapy of mindfulness to be a difficult yet an effective feat for people with the disorder.

Mindfulness is often considered to get in the way of other treatment methodologies for Obsessive-Compulsive Disorder as they, instead of preaching ways of chasing the thoughts, preaches to welcome the thoughts and embrace them for what they are. They are often paired with other treatments like CBT and ERP to enhance their effectiveness. Mindfulness can also be paired with ACT (discussed in the next section) for best results.

This method of therapy works by simply letting the thoughts exist in the mind, no matter how painful they are. The thoughts should not be attached with any judgment or weight and wait until it naturally fades or goes away. This can be incorporated by starting slowly (staring at a low level) and then gradually building it up. The first step towards applying this skill is to have an open mind. Other sets of ways to achieving this skill are:

- Exercising.
- Eating well.
- Find a better balance of work-life.
- Getting ample sleep.
- Maintaining a safe distance from toxic people and the environment.
- Paying attention to the kind of language that the person uses in daily life.
- Minimizing alcohol consumption or stop taking narcotics.
- Letting go of the habit of trying to manipulate intrusive thoughts, and Staying balanced in life.

Obsessive-compulsive disorder (OCD) occurs in numerous ways and is caused by numerous triggers. One such trigger is stress. The best way to enhance your OCD skills is by learning and practicing relaxation techniques on a regular basis. Here are three simple techniques that can be practiced by you.

Deep Breathing

Deep diaphragmatic breathing or "abdominal breathing" sends a very strong relaxation signal to the brain, effectively reducing physiological excitation and thus the level of stress.

The first step in abdominal breathing is to sit or lie down in a quiet position in a quiet room with one hand on your chest and the other on your stomach. Some people are more comfortable with closing their eyes, but it is not necessary. Start with breathing from the nose.

When you breathe in, you should just feel your stomach expand. You will know that you do this well when the hand on your chest is almost stationary and the hand on your stomach moves outwards.

Once you've taken a deep breath, slowly blow air through your pursed lips - like the face you would make if you inflate a balloon - and feel your stomach drop back towards your spine. Again, just the hand over your stomach should move.

Exhaling should take two to three times longer than inhaling. The relaxation that comes with deep breathing takes place after one or two minutes, but takes five, ten, or even 20 minutes to get the most benefits.

Mindfulness Meditation

After you have mastered the deep breathing technique, you can try the mindfulness meditation. Mindfulness meditation is about observing thoughts without judging or rejecting them.

As we practice mindfulness meditation, we become more aware of the thoughts we have and can better detach ourselves from those thoughts. By practicing this technique, we are less likely to be impacted by disturbing thoughts, including obsessions, which are part of an OCD. In fact, mindfulness is an integral part of the treatment of acceptance and commitment.

Start with the deep breathing exercise described earlier to practice mindfulness meditation. When breathing, try to pay attention to the thoughts, feelings, fears, anxiety and worries that go through your head.

Just notice those thoughts and not try to repel them. Notice what happens to these thoughts if you just leave them alone and let go. Use deep breathing as an anchor during this exercise.

It is not uncommon for you to experience a higher level of anxiety at the beginning of mindfulness meditation as it brings you into contact with troubling thoughts, fears, and worries. However, over time, you will feel more at ease to simply sit with these thoughts without taking any action.

Progressive Muscle Relaxation

Progressive Muscle Relaxation (PMR) can also be used with the deep breathing described above. Progressive muscle relaxation can be very useful to identify hidden tension across your body.

To practice PMR, lie down or sit comfortably in a quiet room and start the breathing exercise above. As with your inhalation, tighten all the muscles in your face. Hold the pressure for 10-20 seconds and then release the pressure by exhaling slowly.

Repeat this several times and then gradually work your way across your body - shoulders, arms, stomach, buttocks, legs, calves - and repeat this pattern of inhaling / pressing and exhaling / relaxing.

Let us now understand how mindfulness enhances the CBT method of treating OCD.

Traditional CBT works on improving three major elements or A's. These three A's are acceptance, assessment, and then finally action. The role of mindfulness in them are as follows:

Acceptance - OCD evidently wants the person to live in fear of the inner thoughts that have built a separate inner world for the patients with the disorder. Trying to push these thoughts away from the mind that traps an individual in the fear only goes on to worsen the condition in certain cases.

Thus, accepting and observing the intrusive thoughts, physical sensations, or any other unwanted feeling is a major and first most important step towards bettering the condition. In order to do so, an individual needs to learn to be able to not attach any sort of meaning to these recurrent thoughts or sensations and also be able to stop trying to change them or chase them away.

These can be achieved by being mindful. Now how to achieve these goals through mindfulness? These can be achieved by observing the happenings around you in your day-to-day life. Minute details count in it as well; a person may start by observing the sound of running water while taking a shower to observe minute details like the physical sensation one experiences while being seated in a chair.

Other ways used in mindfulness involve formal meditation that allows a patient to focus on the concept of anchoring. In the case of OCD, the anchoring concept works by focusing on details like their own heartbeat or their breathing pace as the unwanted thoughts start to engulf the mind. By doing these, the cogitation can simply occur and then disappear without the person judging it or attaching any meaning to it. These strategies thus help in the element of acceptance for CBT.

Assessment - Most traditional cognitive-based therapies pivots on finding out the distorted style of thinking that triggers OCD. Mindfulness allows the person to go through the thinking and accept it consensually. For example, it is likely for a person with OCD to have thoughts like, "I am going to get a terrible disease because even after washing my hands once, they are not 100% free from germs".

To mindfully accept a thought would mean to live in this thinking but accept it in a neutral way like "I have washed my hands, but they might not be completely free from germs, so I cannot predict my future now." Simply changing the way of accepting the thinking will prevent the person from performing the compulsions (in our example the compulsion would be washing of hands by the patient repetitively because they want their hands to be completely free from germs).

To be able to mindfully accept certain cogitation, one needs to weigh the seriousness of the thought. People with OCD judge the situation without really focusing on the seriousness of the thought and are trapped in fear of something uncertain. Thus, instead of getting frightened, one first needs to pacify the thoughts by molding them into a neutral perspective.

Action - After successfully accepting and assessing the inner world's thoughts, the ultimate step that remains now is to take necessary and effective action against the OCD. Taking action in traditional CBT generally refers to confronting the thoughts that are fearful and makes them obsessive and perform certain compulsions.

Mindfulness can play a major role in this step as it allows the person to accept unwanted and uneasy thoughts. And as a person can accept the disturbing and uncomfortable scenarios in their imaginary inner world, it becomes much easier for them to stop themselves from performing the compulsive acts.

Why Choose Mindfulness for the Treatment of OCD?

There are several pieces of research on 'mindfulness for OCD' that goes on to show the effectiveness of the therapy for treating OCD. Several researchers have also proven that incorporating mindfulness in treatments for OCD has got better results. Some research works to support the effectiveness of mindfulness in treating OCD are as follows:

- In 2010, three participants with OCD were studied to measure the effectiveness of mindfulness therapy in treating the disorder. These three participants were initially using suppression mechanisms to cope with OCD.

    The suppression mechanism encouraged that instead of accepting the thoughts, they use the coping mechanism where they tried to chase away the uncomfortable thoughts. Each of these three participants was given six sessions each where they were treated using mindfulness-based therapy. After the six sessions, they were studied through an assessment tool named Yale-Brown Obsessive Compulsive Scale.

    This assessment tool is used to measure the presence and severity of symptoms of OCD. The study through Y-BOCS showed that after the mindfulness-based therapy sessions, they were in a much better state than they were in during their earlier days.

- A more recent study in the year 2013 with more number of subjects also showed the effectiveness of this therapy. In this study, 30 patients were involved and were distributed in a heterogeneous group.

  One group was using mindfulness-based skills, whereas the other group was using their coping mechanism. After a while, the study showed that people who were using mindfulness-based skills were found to be performing the compulsions in lesser numbers than the other group whose urge to perform compulsions remain mostly unaltered.

WORKBOOK EXERCISE

Practice mindfulness meditation every day. Start with 5 minutes in the beginning then keep increasing your time. 20 minutes in the morning and 20 minutes in the evening will be perfect but start slow.

Practice progressive muscle relaxation every day. Start with 5 minutes in the beginning then keep increasing your time

ACT – Acceptance and Commitment Therapy

The third wave of behavioral therapy that has existed for a long time now but has recently started getting the limelight in media is ACT or Acceptance and Commitment Therapy. This therapy holds the ability to help with most types of problems, including OCD. It is a form of Mindfulness therapy. Thus, unlike traditional CBTs, ACT helps a patient to recognize and accept their intriguing thinking.

ACT targets six core processes and helps a person deal with the disorder. These are not followed in any particular fashion but are introduced to the patient as and when felt necessary by the psychologist. These six processes are:

- **Cognitive Defusion** - This refers to being able to recognize the imagination or thoughts for what they are and changing the approach towards dealing with them. ACT being a mindfulness-based therapy, does not tell you to skip any thought but to live them and tackle them with a positive approach. The key here is to not try to limit the experiences but to try and change the outlook towards a situation.

- **Acceptance** - Accepting every thought as "just another thought" without giving attaching any weight to them. ACT makes a person learn and practice ways by which they can live through painful or fearful thoughts without trying to avoid them and eventually move forward by being able to not perform the compulsions.

- **Values** - ACT uses various tools that allow the person to figure out the values that are most important and valuable to them. This helps them weigh their thoughts accordingly and makes it crystal clear as to the things that they should focus on. This therapy does not instill values in a person but helps the person to scoop out the values that they already hold, whether consciously or subconsciously.

- **Self as Context** - This is a very interesting step where ACT, through its various procedures, establishes the fact that there is a world outside of the inner world that is created by the mind. This encourages the person with OCD to look beyond their inner experiences and help them recognize that life is not just a sum of our experiences, physical sensations, and intriguing thoughts but much more than that. This step can significantly make a person feel less scared of their thoughts.

- **Commitment or Committed Actions** - The commitment of action refers to considering one's values and working towards achieving them through positive behavior and practices. One should be aware of the fact how behavior can affect us and thereby keep a positive behavior towards life and the surrounding.

- **Contact With Present Time** - This step directs a person towards accepting the fact that the future can neither be correctly predicted nor can it be altered. The only way to deal with the anxiety about what will happen in the future is to live in the present and experience every single detail without trying to infer anything from it.

ACT therapy does not focus on the thoughts and the working of the mind but on how to deal with them and the many approaches following which the intriguing notions can be dealt with positively. It does not involve any sort of exposure exercises rather includes exercises that allow the patient to be open to acceptance and pave a path towards a positive life through mindful choices.

Why Choose Acceptance and Commitment Therapy for the Treatment of OCD?

A study that has successfully proven the effectiveness of ACT therapy is:-

In the year 2006, a study by Twohig et al. explored the effectiveness of the therapy by first treating the subjects with the therapy.

After successfully imparting the therapy, reports showed that the participants were found less intrigued to perform compulsions. They were also found with a lesser need to try to avoid or distract themselves from the intriguing notions and were less obsessive. After

ACT was successfully carried out, it was found that the patients were less anxious or depressed.

To date, ERP is considered the standard technique to help patients deal with OCD, but some patients may not respond to this treatment at all. Therefore alternatives to this like mindfulness-based therapy and Acceptance and Commitment Therapy (ACT) are the need of the hour.

There is a circumstantial amount of evidence that shows these techniques can effectively treat OCD (although a major number of studies have been carried out on a less number of subjects). These treatment mechanisms require practice over time, but once they have been successfully carried out, they are sure to significantly reduce the urge for carrying out compulsions in the patients.

WORKBOOK EXERCISE

Accepting Emotions

When you experience an uncomfortable emotion, the first step is to take a few slow, deep breaths and quickly scan your body from head to toe.

You will likely experience some uncomfortable sensations. Searching for the strong feeling - the one that annoys you the most. For example, this may be a lump in the throat, a knot in the stomach, or pain in the chest.

Focus your attention on how it feels. Watch it curiously, as if you were a friendly scientist, discovering another interesting phenomenon.

Pay attention to the sensation. Note where it begins and where it ends. Find out as much as you can. If you had to draw a line around the feeling, what would the outline be? Is it on the surface of the body or inside yourself or both? How far inside is this going? Where do you get the most intense feeling? Where does the weakest one go? How does that differ in the middle and the edges? Is it pulsating or vibrating? Is it light or heavy? In motion or still? What is its temperature?

Take some deeper breaths and let the fight go with this feeling. Breathe in. Imagine that you are breathing in and around it. • Make space for it. Loosen up around it. And you don't have to like it or want it. Just let it be.

The idea is to watch the sensation - not think about it. When your mind starts commenting on what's going on, just say "Thank you, mind!" And come back to observe. • You may find that challenging. You can have a strong desire to fight or retain it. If that is the case, recognise it and do not give in. (Recognition is a bit like nodding your head in appreciation, as if to say, "There you are. I see you.") When you have recognised this need, return to the sensation itself.

Do not attempt to get rid of the sensation or attempt to alter it. If it changes on its own, that's okay. If it hasn't changed, it will. The intention is not to amend or eliminate it. • You may need to concentrate on this feeling for a few seconds or minutes before fully letting go. Be patient. Use as much time as you need. You're learning something valuable.

Once you have done this, scan your body again and see if you have another strong feeling which bothers you. If yes, use this process again. You may do so with as many different sensations as you wish. Continue until you feel as if you have no more problems with your feelings.

During this exercise, two things will happen: either your feelings will change or they will remain the same. None of that matters. This exercise is not meant to alter your feelings. This is about acceptance.

4 quick steps to emotional acceptance

OBSERVE. Recognize the feelings within your body.

TO BREATHE. Take a few deep breaths. Breathe into and around them.

EXPAND. Make room for those emotions. Create space for them.

ALLOW. Let them be here. Make peace with them

Chapter 10: Other Methods of Treatment

OCD can be treated very successfully with comprehensive treatment procedures like any kind of residential treatment program or intensive outpatient programs where the ERP therapy principles are emphasized. Another treatment method that can be very helpful in the case of Obsessive-Compulsive Disorder is that of Deep Brain Stimulation or what is known as the DBS procedures.

This might be used for patients who have stopped responding to traditional approaches of treatment. What happens, in this case, is that electrodes are implanted in the patient's brain to garner proper responses to impulses. The other mode of treatment that is very helpful in the case of Obsessive-Compulsive Disorder is that of TMS or what can also be referred to as Transcranial Magnetic Stimulation.

This method is used in people above the age of 22 and goes up to the age of 68 mostly. This is a non-invasive method of treatment that takes the help of magnetic fields in order to stimulate the nerve cells in the brain, and along with that, an electromagnetic coil is placed alongside the patient's scalp near one's forehead. What happens then is that a magnetic pulse gets delivered by the electromagnet present, which in turn gets the nerve cells stimulated in the brain.

So far, we have discussed the different methods of treating Obsessive-Compulsive disorder. But that being said, it is strictly advised to consult one's doctor at the earliest if one feels that there is a need for taking medicines or undergoing any kind of treatment. The most important thing, however, is to not avoid any symptoms of OCD that might occur in a person.

It is imperative to not take one's mental health for granted and give it its all due importance in the proper time so that things can be tackled when there is still time and the symptoms don't get time to intensify with time. So, have a conversation with your doctor at the earliest and understand all the necessary dos and don'ts in case you need any treatment.

Chapter 11: How to Sustain It for the Long-Term and Not Fall Back?

Now that you have comprehensive knowledge about OCD and how it can be treated, we come to the final chapter, where I will be giving you some easy tips to sustain your recovery and not fall back into your previous state. Remember that if you think things are going pretty well, OCD can be triggered by the simplest of things and hijack your entire routine ahead. And along with that, the most common thing that will come rushing in is anxiety.

Once you face this, it can take a huge chunk of your time and energy to overcome it. OCD is referred to as a lifelong condition, and it can be kept in control through therapy and medication. But a very good way of keeping it in check and not allowing yourself to fall back is through self-care, and in this chapter, I will share some tips as to how you can do that.

Eat Good Food

You need to take good care of your nutrition. And it is not only about one random day. You might wake up and decide that you are going to eat healthy today. What about the rest of the days in a week? If you eat nutritious and healthy food on all days and keep it up regularly, only then will you be able to reap the benefits. A wholesome diet has been found to be very good to sustain your OCD recovery. For this you need –

Protein – There are so many neurotransmitters in your brain that are boosted by the breakdown of good protein. For example, Gamma-Aminobutyric acid, which is popularly known as GABA, is enhanced when you intake the right amount of protein. This neurotransmitter is known to calm down your revved up and excited brain, which makes it so important for OCD patients.

Moreover, you all probably know about serotonin which is also commonly known as the happy hormone. When you eat proteinaceous foods, it delivers tryptophan in your body, which is associated with serotonin (it has been found that OCD patients have very low amounts of serotonin in their body).

And then, protein intake also regularizes the levels of dopamine because this particular compound is derived from phenylalanine (an amino acid). Most of the imbalances of the brain are somehow related to these three neurotransmitters, and OCD is no different.

Some common protein sources that you should include are legumes, seeds, nuts, seafood, poultry, eggs, and grass-fed or organic meats. If you are someone who is currently following the trend of being vegan and you are also recovering from OCD, it is of crucial importance that you maintain proper protein intake so that your neurotransmitter levels remain balanced.

Good Fats – The inclusion of good-quality fats in your diet is as important as protein. These fats are usually present in seeds, nuts, olive oil, coconut oil, grass-fed animal meats, avocado, ghee, and also food items rich in omega-3-fatty acids like salmon, sardines, mackerel, chia seeds, and flaxseed.

But are you wondering why these are important for enhancing your mental health? Well, the reason is quite simple – approximately 60% of the human brain is made up of fats! Your brain messages are carried by neurons, and their formation depends on fats.

The fats also help in improving the performance of the brain and also make its integrity better. Apart from this, you also get relief from inflammation due to good fats.

But, at the same time, you must also keep in mind that when you are increasing the consumption of good fats, you should simultaneously cut down on the consumption of harmful fats that is present in packaged foods and baked goods.

Fresh Vegetables and Fruits – Next, we come to another group of very important food items that you should not leave out – fresh vegetables and fruits. These are essential for your body because of the micronutrients that they provide.

They not only help you carry out several essential chemical reactions throughout the day but also assist in keeping your brain healthy. For starters, you should increase your intake of magnesium, zinc, vitamin C, and most importantly, B vitamins. Always prefer organic fruits and vegetables and try to include them in every meal you have!

Another small tip that I can give you is that you should avoid any stimulants like coffee, tea, soda, or anything that has caffeine in it because it can easily elevate your levels of anxiety.

Don't Avoid Your Fears

It is important for OCD patients that they do not avoid what they fear. Avoidance will only cause more triggers. The more you try to take a shortcut around your fears, obsessive-compulsive thoughts will start creeping in. So, the most common advice to people who are trying to sustain their recovery is that you should face your fears.

Expose yourself to the things that are triggering you, and then work on delaying the arousal of any type of compulsive behavior. In the beginning, you might find yourself performing the ritual nonetheless. Even if that happens, there is no need to beat yourself upon it. You can simply reduce your time spent on that particular ritual. The idea behind this process is that the more you expose yourself to your triggers, it will become a usual thing for you, and you will no longer feel anxious over time. The less anxious you feel, the more control you will have in general.

Another thing to keep in mind is that you should always expect that an obsessive thought might strike you at any moment. When you have this type of mindset, you will not be thrown off balance even when the thought strikes. You will be better prepared to use all the tools you learned in your therapy sessions. But if you always are in fear and keep telling yourself that these thoughts are not going to come, then you are lying, and when they do come, you will be at a complete loss and not know what to do.

Risk is present in every aspect of life – even when you are recovering from OCD – so, no matter how much you try, you can never really get rid of risk completely. Once you accept that, sustaining a normal life while having OCD will become much easier.

Also, some people try to seek reassurance from their close ones or even from themselves just because they are afraid to face their reality. Never do that. What you should do is accept your reality and tell yourself what lies ahead of you or what has already happened to you. Whatever good effects therapy is having upon you, reassurance will only cancel out all of that and be a hindrance in your path of improvement. No matter what reasons you use to justify the habit of seeking reassurance, at the end of the day, it is nothing but another form of compulsion.

So, even if you are facing compulsive or obsessive thoughts from time to time, it is better that you do not try to analyze or argue with them. You simply need to accept those thoughts and tell yourself that they are real. The more time you will waste behind avoiding these thoughts, the more you will walk away from recovery. Avoidance usually has the opposite effect on OCD because patients start thinking about those things with greater intensity.

Don't Be a Black-and-White Thinker

When you are recovering from OCD, there will be times when you will slip up, and that's completely okay! You don't need to beat yourself up about such one or two instances. You don't need to tell yourself that you are a complete failure just because you let your compulsive thoughts in once. If you do have the urge to give in to compulsion, you can try doing something else so that you can cancel it. Remind yourself that you are not going anywhere and that you are here for the long haul, so second chances will keep coming in.

When a person is learning something new, they make mistakes. It is the same for you. Living with OCD and recovering from it is something new for you. When it comes to therapy, everyone makes mistakes, and this is a normal thing. You need to learn to accept it. Never let a setback throw you off balance. Just keep telling yourself that a single setback does not have the power to send you back to square one because it can't take away all the skills that you have learned. You cannot really forget all those lessons and coping skills that therapy has taught you. Tomorrow is a new day, and you can always start over.

Follow Your Prescriptions

The next most important thing to sustain your recovery and not fall back is to stick to the prescriptions that your doctor suggested. It is of utmost importance that you take your medications on time. It is true that alcohol and drugs can be very tempting to indulge in, but even though you might feel relieved for a moment, they are triggers in the long run.

At first, when you take that first sip of alcohol, you will feel as if your anxiety is seeping away – but remember, that is only momentary. There is no shortcut to deal with OCD. Medication and therapy are the only effective methods. Before that alcohol totally leaves your system, it will give birth to more and more anxiety. The same thing happens when you smoke cigarettes because of the nicotine content in them that acts in the same way as alcohol.

Be Patience With Your Progress

Good things take time, and they don't certainly happen overnight. Remind yourself that whenever you start feeling impatient about your progress and you feel like you are not doing enough. Everyone walks on their path of progress at their own pace. Just because someone you know has faster progress than you doesn't mean that you will have the same.

You need to keep faith in yourself and simply focus on one day at a time. Do all the homework that your therapist has suggested and complete the things you planned for the day. Set micro-goals and complete them. This is how you will see progress in the long run.

Another important thing to keep in mind is that you need to review your progress and assignments from time to time. Even if you think that you have it all in your mind, it's not enough – you need to go through it. Sometimes, it is easy for the human mind to forget about assignments that you don't love, and that's how you overlook important things if you don't go over them.

Talk to Your Therapist If You Face Problems With an Assignment

Every OCD patient has to go through certain assignments on a daily basis. Your therapist will keep updating these assignments and give you new ones depending on your progress or current situation. But at times, it might so happen that you have been given an assignment that you don't feel like doing.

If that's the case with you, you should make an appointment with your therapist and talk to him/her about this. Don't suppress the issue – it will never do you any good. It is your own therapy, and so, you have every right to say the things that you are feeling, or if you are not comfortable about something, you should be vocal about that as well.

The ultimate aim of every assignment that the therapist gives you is to create a small amount of anxiety within you that you can withstand. Its aim is never to overwhelm you. Your therapist will never want you to suffer because of an assignment or face a setback. Similarly, you should also be open to stretch your limits a little bit more with every assignment because that's how you make progress.

Some OCD patients take up too much time to start on their assignments. They think that they are waiting for the perfect moment, but as the old saying goes – the perfect moment to start is now! The more you think you are going to find a certain moment to start with it, the more you will procrastinate, and people with OCD often face procrastination to a great extent.

So, a solution to this is that you should make it a habit of starting on your assignments the day you receive them – in this way, you will be able to beat procrastination. Before each day starts, make it a habit of going through your assignments for the day. You might think you remember them all by heart, but even if you forget a small detail, it will not go the way your therapist planned.

Maintain a Journal

When you undergo treatment for OCD, there will be some strategies that work in an excellent manner, and there will be those that don't seem to work at all. If you want to keep track of what works for you and what doesn't, the best way to do it is to maintain a journal.

This will keep all your successful efforts in one place so that even if you feel particularly bad on some days, you can always revisit your journal and follow the steps that helped a lot in the past.

Your journal does not have to be something fancy. The main aim is to keep note of all the important points that helped in your recovery. When you have it written down, it will serve you in the future in moments when you find it hard to remember on your own. Whenever you feel lost, you can always check back on your journal to find out what helped you the previous time. But most importantly, a journal also reminds you of your success against OCD and gives you confidence on days when you feel low.

When days get tough, your journal will always help you to shift your focus to things that will make life easier and not let the compulsive thoughts creep in. Your list of successes will keep increasing with time, and this will make you even more proud and confident.

An important thing to keep in mind here is that you should only keep track of your successes and not your failures. There are times in life when you have to cut yourself some slack and give yourself a pat on the back. You need to appreciate yourself whenever you do something well and apply the coping strategies correctly. This will give you encouragement and keep pushing you in the right direction.

You might not realize the benefits of the journal in the short run, but as time goes on, you will see how miraculously the journal can help you. It will help you see how far you have come and overcome your OCD, and this will boost your self-esteem and confidence further so that you fight even harder and sustain your recovery.

Avoid Chasing Perfectionism

For OCD patients, perfectionism is something most people suffer from. But your aim should be not to allow yourself to get side-tracked by it. Sometimes you might find your mind telling you that if you want to recover, you need to get everything right; otherwise, things will not be the way you want them to, and this means that you have to be perfect while doing your homework assignments.

But does it really work that way? No! The more you are concentrated on doing things the perfect way, the more you are at risk of developing it as a compulsive behavior pattern.

So, how will you identify that you are chasing perfectionism? Watch out for instances where you are too rigid about rules and doing things the same way every time to achieve a certain level of perfection.

Another thing that I'd like to tell you is that you should avoid taking up your whole day just to complete your assignment. Remember that the assignment should be only a part of your life and not take it up entirely. You need to live your life too and enjoy it the way you want.

But when you are trying to avoid perfectionism, you shouldn't give in to thoughts like 'it's only an assignment' and 'it doesn't matter in real life.' Your assignment is meant for your benefit. If you do it with the mentality that you are completing it just because your therapist asked you to, then it's not going to work. You need to do it willingly and also understand everything.

When you are doing your assignment, pay full attention to it. Don't let your mind wander off or tune out for a while. That's only harmful and will not bring any good results. Your mind tries to tune out because it wants to avoid the anxiety. But you should try to face the anxiety instead of avoiding it.

A good remedy is to solely focus on your assignment when you are doing it. Don't do any other distracting activity at the time. You fear your anxiety, and so, you need to build a tolerance towards it rather than running away from it. And if you want that to happen, you cannot zone out – you need to be present at the moment.

If the assignment seems hard, don't shove it away, saying that it does you no good. Always look at it as a learning opportunity and tell yourself that the universe is only giving you another chance to come out stronger and practice more.

When you are doing your assignment, take your time. Don't rush through it just to get it done and avoid your anxiety altogether. See your assignment in a good light that is going to help you get better. Your goal is not to finish it as fast as possible but to allow a moderate level of anxiety to seep into your mind so that you can increase your level of tolerance towards it.

At the same time, if you are doing your assignment well and good and it is not giving you any anxiety at all, you need to report it to your therapist. But before letting the therapist know, do your assignment for at least a week or two and if the same thing continues, let them know. There are some assignments that might not spark anxiety in you instantly but cause it later.

I would also like to remind you that whenever you suffer from anxiety attacks, tell yourself that the anxiety is not what the root problem is. You need to deal with your compulsive thoughts, and the anxiety will go away along with that.

So, these were some of the steps that you can take to not fall back on your recovery and stay strong. Overall, remember that OCD might not make sense a lot of times. If you are feeling confused or not sure about what to do, consult your therapist right away and do what they suggest. They will always tell you the best possible course of action.

Conclusion

Thank you for making it through to the end of *this book*; let's hope it was informative and able to provide you with all of the tools you need to achieve your goals, whatever they may be.

Always remember that knowledge is power, and I hope this book has been able to enlighten you about OCD and made you more aware of the subject than you previously were. If you follow the advice given in this book and read every chapter from the beginning until the end, then you are surely going to benefit from this.

So, I know what you might be thinking now. Will recovery be easy? The answer is no; it won't be. This is mostly because there are so many unhealthy and unhelpful habits that you need to unlearn, but you need to take it one day at a time. Recovery doesn't happen overnight. But if you don't take that first step, it won't ever happen.

When you start walking on the path of recovery, you will soon understand that it is about changing your narrative and developing a different kind of relationship with your thoughts where they no longer scare you or rule your life. They will not be able to torment you. Once that happens, you'll know that you have done it and you have been successful at taming your OCD.

Finally, if you found this book useful in any way, a review is always appreciated!

About Author

Mike Abraham is a psychotherapist in private practice specializing in the treatment of obsessive-compulsive disorder (OCD) and related disorders. He has been practicing meditation and mindfulness for many years, and has a special interest in the integration of mindfulness and self-compassion principles with cognitive behavioral therapy (CBT) for OCD, anxiety disorders, and eating disorders.

WORKBOOK EXERCISE

Journal

www.ingramcontent.com/pod-product-compliance
Lightning Source LLC
LaVergne TN
LVHW041840070526
838199LV00045BA/1371